D1201378

Criminal Justice
Recent Scholarship

Edited by
Marilyn McShane and Frank P. Williams III

A Series from LFB Scholarly

Domestic Violence
Legal Sanctions and Recidivism Rates among Male Perpetrators

S. Deborah Cosimo

LFB Scholarly Publishing LLC
El Paso 2012

Library of Congress Cataloging-in-Publication Data

Cosimo, S. Deborah, 1951-
  Domestic violence : legal sanctions and recidivism rates among male perpetrators / S. Deborah Cosimo.
    p. cm.
  Includes bibliographical references and index.
  ISBN 978-1-59332-488-9 (hardcover : alk. paper)
  1. Family violence--Texas. 2. Family violence--Texas--Prevention. 3. Family violence--Law and legislation--Texas. 4. Abusive men--Texas. 5. Recidivists--Texas. I. Title.
  HV6626.22.T4C67 2012
  364.15'55--dc23
                                    2011031213

ISBN 978-1-59332-488-9

Printed on acid-free 250-year-life paper.

Manufactured in the United States of America.

Table of Contents

v

List of Tables

List of Figures

Acknowledgements

I dedicate this book to the memory of T. G., whose husband abused her for many years. He experienced numerous encounters with law enforcement, yet the courts did not impose any sanctions for his violent actions towards T. G. None, that is, until he murdered her.

I would like to express my deep appreciation to the following persons for their support and encouragement: Barney Cosimo, Daniel Rodeheaver, Valli Hatzes, Kevin Yoder, Nicole Dash, James Williams, Lisa Muftić, Barbara Rodman, Gerry Veeder, Rob Miller, and Edward Gondolf.

Finally, although I am an employee of the Federal government, the views expressed in this book do not represent the government of the United States, or the Department of Health and Human Services, Office of the Inspector General, Office of Evaluation and Inspections.

CHAPTER ONE

Introduction

Whether communities define domestic violence as personal trouble, public issue, or both, the everyday environments for victims of domestic violence demand immediate attention. According to a statewide survey conducted for the Texas Council on Family Violence in 2002, Texans consider domestic violence a serious problem (Saurage, 2003). With an estimated prevalence rate of 6 out of 1,000 adults in Texas reporting domestic violence to local law enforcement in 2000, approximately 74% of 1,272 respondents in this survey indicated that they or someone they knew experienced some form of domestic violence in their lifetime (Saurage, 2003; Texas Department of Public Safety, 2000; United States Census Bureau, 2000). Most of the survey respondents, however, demonstrated a willingness to blame the abuse on the victims and considered domestic violence the result of circumstances beyond the batterer's control (Saurage, 2003). Although public perceptions may connect the causes of violence to circumstances beyond individual control, the principle of holding batterers accountable for their behavioral choices is critical to intervention in domestic violence cases. How, then, does a community hold batterers accountable?

Many communities have developed an indigenous framework of institutions that intervene in domestic violence (Shepard & Pence, 1999). Against the backdrop of a Texas county that defines domestic violence as a public issue of social structure, this study examines the impact of legal sanctions upon the recidivism rates of men who commit domestic violence. It explores one aspect of a community holding batterers accountable through imposing civil and criminal sanctions for

1

domestic violence related offenses. Specifically, this research examines the impact of legal sanctions upon the relative risk of recidivism of men who are involved with the civil and criminal courts for domestic violence related offenses, defined as offenses committed against a female intimate partner. All men in the sample were court ordered to attend a battering intervention program.

The unit of analysis for this study is males who commit domestic violence assault in a large, mostly urban county in Texas (hereafter referred to as "the county"). It is well documented that women commit the crime of domestic violence (Bair-Merritt, Crowne, Thompson, et al., 2010, Gover, Jennings, Davis, Tomsich, & Tewksbury, 2011; Hines & Douglas, 2009). Mandatory arrest and prosecution policies in particular have drawn more women into the criminal justice system as offenders (Hamilton & Worthen, 2011; Rajan & McCloskey, 2007). Although some argue that domestic violence is a more gender-neutral concept than earlier work in this area suggested (Straus, 2009), this study deals with men as the perpetrators, for reasons explained in Chapter Three.

This study examines the influence of civil and criminal legal sanctions or dose-responses upon the risk of recidivism of domestic violence over a period extending from the date of the initial case (hereinafter referred to as the "index case") until December 31, 2006. For the purposes of this study, the term "legal sanctions" is defined as activities that are carried out the county in response to domestic violence offenses, including civil protective orders, arrest, probation, revocation of probation, and incarceration.

Prior research on recidivism of men who abuse their intimate partners and are court ordered to battering intervention programs focuses primarily on comparing battering intervention program completers and non-completers (Babcock & Steiner, 1999; Bennett, Stoops, Call, & Flett, 2007; Bowen, Gilchrist, & Beech, 2005; Cissner & Puffett, 2006; Gondolf, 2004; Gordon & Moriarty, 2003; Gover, et al., 2011; Hendricks, Werner, Shipway, & Turinetti, 2006; Jewell & Wormith, 2010; MacLeod, Pi, Smith & Rose-Goodwin, 2009; Maxwell, Davis, & Taylor, 2010; Olver, Stockdale, & Wormith; Petrucci, 2010; Sartin, Hansen, & Huss, 2006). Research findings typically attribute recidivism or non-recidivism of domestic violence to treatment effects of the battering intervention program. However, the efforts of law enforcement, the justice system, and probation confound the effect size of the program (Babcock, Green, & Robie, 2004). Rather than focusing on battering intervention programs as the sole arbiter of accountability, this research explores three factors not addressed currently in the literature on men who batter women, and who are court ordered to battering intervention programs. These factors are the impact of cumulative civil and criminal legal sanctions imposed in response to a single offense of domestic violence and recidivism of domestic violence related offenses, the opportunity to recidivate, and if legal sanctions have an effect on how long a man maintains his non-recidivism status. Additionally, this study defines domestic violence broadly. Rather than limiting the offense to assault upon an intimate partner, this study defines domestic violence as any offense directed toward an intimate partner, but not typically included in operational definitions of domestic violence in the literature on men who batter (Townsend, Hunt, Kuck, & Baxter, 2006). These offenses include such crimes as sexual assault, stalking, kidnapping, retaliation, criminal trespass, terroristic threats, and burglary.

LEGAL SANCTIONS

Victims of domestic violence who are granted civil protective orders experience high levels of abuse ranging from sexual assault, threatened or injured with a weapon, physical assault, and choking to slapping, kicking, and shoving (Keilitz, Hannaford, & Efkeman, 1997, Kethineni & Beichner, 2009; Klein, 2008). However, prior research related to recidivism of domestic violence has primarily concentrated on criminal cases, rather than civil protective orders (Bouffard & Muftić, 2007; Davis, Smith, & Nickles, 1998; Gondolf, 2002; Gover, et al., 2011; Kingsnorth, 2006; Murphy, Musser, & Maton, 1998; Petrucci, 2010; Rempel, Labriola, & Davis, 2008; Salazar, Emshoff, Baker, and Crowley, 2007; Wilson & Klein, 2006). Because the impact of domestic violence offenses on victims could be as severe in civil protective order cases as it is in criminal cases, this research considers the county's response to domestic violence through civil and criminal court sanctions that could be imposed for a single offense. Therefore, legal sanctions imposed for domestic violence offenses by the county could include arrest (Manning, 1993; Salazar et al., 2007; Sherman & Berk, 1984), civil protective orders (Keilitz, Hannaford, & Efkeman,

1997; Kethineni & Beichner, 2009; Logan, Shannon, Walker, & Faragher, 2006), community supervision through probation (Klein & Crowe, 2008), and incarceration (Salazar et al., 2007; Ulmer, 2001). This study uses an index designed to measure the cumulative effects, or dose-response, of legal sanctions on the case that resulted in a court mandate to participate in a battering intervention program in the county in 2001.

REDUCED OPPORTUNITIES TO RECIDIVATE

Prior domestic violence research has not explored reduced opportunities due to incarceration as a factor in recidivism of domestic violence. Incapacitation in the form of time spent in jail or prison during the follow-up period has an effect on an offender's opportunity for recidivism. For example, if a man is incarcerated for a considerable amount of time during the follow-up period, the absence of recidivism could be the direct impact of incapacitation, rather than any effects from the sanctions imposed at the time of the original case (Brennan & Mednick, 1994; MacLeod et al., 2009; Tollefson & Gross, 2006). Court involvement for non-domestic violence related cases during the follow-up period may also result in additional convictions and incarceration for other crimes, thus reducing the opportunity for recidivism of domestic violence (Forde & Kennedy, 1997; Wooldredge, 2007). To determine if incarceration diminishes opportunities for recidivism, this study examines risk of recidivism and incarceration for any offense during the follow-up period.

LENGTH OF TIME AND RECIDIVISM

How long a man is able to "survive" or maintain his non-recidivism status after community intervention for domestic violence is of interest to researchers (Bowen, Gilchrist, & Beech, 2005; Cissner & Puffett, 2006; Klein & Crowe, 2008; Rempel, Labriola, & Davis, 2008; Wilson & Klein, 2006; Wooldredge & Thistlethwaite, 2005). Hence, this study employs the Cox proportional hazards regression model, using recidivism as the status variable and the time spent without committing domestic violence related offenses as the time variable. Using Cox proportional hazards regression, researchers have studied the risk of recidivism and variables such as age (Davis, Taylor, Maxwell, 2000; McCarroll et al., 2000; Wilson & Klein, 2006), race or ethnicity (Case,

2008; Davis, Taylor, Maxwell, 2000; McCarroll, et al., 2000), probation (Klein & Crowe, 2008), prior criminal history for domestic violence (Davis, Taylor, & Maxwell, 2000; Klein & Crowe, 2008) and prior criminal history for non-domestic violence related offenses (Klein & Crowe, 2008; Wilson & Klein, 2006). However, prior research has not explored whether the number of sanctions imposed has an effect on how long a man maintains his non-recidivism status for domestic violence related offenses. Therefore, using an index designed to measure the cumulative effect (or dose-response) of legal sanctions, this study examines the relative risk of recidivism, and the number of sanctions imposed for the specific case that resulted in a court mandate to participate in a battering intervention program in the county in 2001.

BOOK OUTLINE

As noted, this book presents research that examines the impact of legal sanctions upon the relative risk of recidivism of men who are involved with the civil and criminal courts for domestic violence related offenses.

The definition of a problem influences perception and shapes interventions designed to solve the problem (Cosimo, 1999; Stone, 2002). Chapter Two provides a context for legal sanctions and the criminalization of domestic violence, discussing the intersection of history, politics, personal troubles, and public issues (Brewer, 2003; Mills, 1959/2000).

Chapter Three explores sociological theoretical perspectives on domestic violence, within the context of personal troubles and public issues. It discusses four theoretical perspectives that inform criminal justice responses to domestic violence: social exchange/deterrence, social learning, feminist theory, and the ecological framework (Danis, 2003). The chapter examines the application of each of these theories to legal sanctions for domestic violence.

Chapter Four explains the rationale and describes the methods and data used to examine the impact of legal sanctions on recidivism rates among perpetrators of domestic violence in the county over a five-year period. It describes the research design, data sources, sampling frame, dependent and independent variables, hypotheses, and analysis. Finally, the chapter discusses the limitations of the data and methods used for this research.

Chapter Five presents the characteristics of the 607 men included in the study. These characteristics include age, race, prior court involvement, post-index case court involvement, battering intervention program hours, and the amount of time spent incarcerated during the follow-up period after the offense for which the court ordered sanction included referral to battering intervention in 2001.

Chapter Six describes the men in the sample who met the criteria for recidivism of domestic violence, and draws comparisons to those who did not have any domestic violence related cases filed during the follow-up period. Additionally, the chapter examines variables that may significantly influence recidivism rates.

Chapter Seven discusses the analyses results and compares these results to prior research on domestic violence, legal sanctions, and recidivism rates. This chapter explores possible explanations for the 30% recidivism rate found among the men in the sample.

Finally, Chapter Eight summarizes the findings of this study and discusses the implications for future research on legal sanctions and recidivism of domestic violence.

CHAPTER TWO

Domestic Violence: Personal Trouble or Public Issue?

A distinction exists between the "personal troubles of milieu" and "public issues of social structure." Troubles are a private matter, occurring within the character of the individual and in relationships with others. Personal values held by the individual are threatened. Issues are a public matter where some value held in esteem by the public is threatened. Issues are located within the social and historical institutions of a society (Mills, 1959/2000). Problem or issue definition shapes public perception, public policy, and intervention (Cosimo, 1999; Foster-Fishman, Nowell, & Yang, 2007; Olivero, 2010; Stone, 2002, Weiss, 1989). Some interventions are more meaningful depending on whether the focus is on the individual perceived to have a personal trouble or problem, the social structure that fosters social values that support the behavior, or the interaction of both (O'Neill, 2005; Portwood & Heany, 2007). Equally important is to link history and politics, giving a wider context to individuals within society (Brewer, 2003; Mills, 1959/2000).

Vacillation between defining domestic violence as personal trouble or public issue is evident in historical and political efforts to address domestic violence in the United States. It is commonly thought that advocates for battered women identified domestic violence as a public issue in the 1960's. In fact, there were earlier periods of social reform that addressed domestic violence (Bailey, 2006; Pleck, 1989). The belief that the need to enforce domestic violence laws outweighs the traditional rights of husbands or respect for domestic privacy is necessary but not sufficient for reform, as demonstrated in the history of criminalization of domestic violence in the United States (Pleck, 1989).

The history of criminalization of domestic violence has its roots in the English common law doctrine of coverture. The doctrine of coverture legitimized a man's authority to use violence to control his wife because he was responsible for her behavior (Bevacqua & Baker, 2004). In the New England colonies, the community of Puritans addressed domestic violence as early as the 1640s. Puritans believed the family was the expression of religious values and central to a life of piety. The religious community of Puritans defined "wicked carriage," or domestic violence and child abuse, as sin and a threat to social order; the family could not be a sanctuary for violence, and the pious life transcended the privacy of the family. Neighbors watched out for each other to ensure that the sins of a few would not jeopardize the status of the community in the eyes of God (Pleck, 1989; 2004). In 1641, Puritans in the Massachusetts Bay Colony enacted the *Body of Liberties*, including the first law in the world that criminalized domestic violence (Buzawa & Buzawa, 2003; Pleck, 1989). Plymouth Colony followed suit in 1672.

According to the *Body of Liberties*, "Everie marryed woeman shall be free from bodilie correction or stripes by her husband, unlesse it be in his owne defence upon her assalt" [sic] (Massachusetts, 1890, p. 51). Nonetheless, the purpose of laws against domestic violence was largely symbolic. They drew a line between saint and sinner, demonstrated vigilance against sin to God and the community, and supported the hierarchy within the household and civil society (Pleck, 1989). They were rarely enforced. When they were, punishments were lenient (Bailey, 2006; Pleck, 1989). It was enough, magistrates believed, that the disgrace inherent in punishment and "holy watching" by the community acted as a deterrent to further violence (Pleck, 1989). Over time, the limited enforcement of domestic violence laws decreased significantly. Between 1663 and 1682, there were four complaints of wife abuse in Plymouth. The cases dwindled to one complaint every ten years until 1702. For the first fifty years of the eighteenth century, there were no accusations of wife abuse in Plymouth. The belief that the community was responsible for regulating activity that occurred in private waned and the Puritan model of a community engaged in "holy watching" began to fade. Communities no longer considered domestic violence a threat to social order and viewed the family as a private institution, defining domestic violence as personal trouble for the next hundred years (Pleck, 1989; 2004).

Although the state approached domestic violence as a personal trouble, John Stuart Mill argued in 1859 that the state has an obligation to exercise power over an individual to prevent harm to others. Concerned with the tyrannical power of husbands over wives, Mill observed that the state disregarded this obligation in the case of families. He noted that men were able to obtain a victim through the law of marriage, abusing the institution and creating human misery. Mill reasoned that wives should have the same rights and enjoy the same protection under the law as all others (Mill, 1859/1975; Mill, 1869/1970). The doctrine of chastisement, which upheld the right of a man to discipline his wife, impeded the criminalization of domestic violence between 1750 and 1874. Heightened respect for privacy, decreased enthusiasm for state intervention, and belief in the sanctity of the family protected the home from public view and state intervention (Pleck, 1989).

While legislatures passed no laws criminalizing domestic violence between 1672 and 1850, domestic violence was treated as a crime though complaints heard by local city courts. Courts established the doctrine of chastisement through three appellate court rulings issued between 1824 and 1868. *Bradley v. State* 1 Miss. 156 (1824) upheld a man's right to chastise moderately his wife. *State v. Black*, 60 N.C. 266 (1864) upheld the right of a husband to use necessary force and concluded that courts should intervene only in cases of permanent injury or excessive violence or cruelty. Finally, in *State v. Rhodes*, 61 N.C. 453 (1868), the North Carolina Supreme Court rejected the premise that a husband has the right to use force to discipline his wife, but ruled that it would not interfere with family relations in "trifling" cases (Bailey, 2006; Bevacqua & Baker, 2004; Pleck, 1989).

The call for increased criminal sanctions for domestic violence gained momentum during the major social upheavals in the late nineteenth century. The focus shifted from personal trouble within the family to public issue, defining domestic violence once more as an indicator of social morality. There were several reasons. First, the post-Civil War climate led to increased public acceptance of the state's responsibility to enforce public morality and intervene in family affairs when necessary. Like the Puritans, the prevailing belief was that a society that did not uphold the moral law would decay. Second, the public was afraid of crime, leading to a more serious approach to domestic violence. Third, the fear of violent crime connected to a desire to impose Protestant morality on an industrial society. In contrast to the Puritan belief in wicked carriage, however, the enemy of society was not the sinner; the enemy was the "dangerous classes," which included new immigrants and lower social classes. At a time of severe economic depression, industrialization created large numbers of vagabonds, tramps, and thieves that threatened to disrupt the social order. The potential of large groups of unemployed and the threat of a permanent criminal class invigorated the demand for criminalization of domestic violence (Buzawa & Buzawa, 2003; Pleck, 1989; Pleck, 2004). Finally, women began to achieve a modicum of financial freedom, including protection of their property rights and the gradual acceptance of women working outside the home in service related jobs (Buzawa & Buzawa, 2003).

During this period, the courts largely discredited the doctrine of chastisement as a defense for domestic violence. Motivated by a desire to create a single standard of morality, three ideological sources guided reform: law enforcement, feminism, and the temperance movement (Pleck, 1989).

Law enforcement sought to punish domestic violence as a serious crime. Proponents of criminal sanctions argued that fines and imprisonment were not effective. They argued for instituting corporal punishment as a means to hold men who abused their wives accountable for their behavior (Pleck, 1989, 2004). In their zeal to bring law and order, twelve states considered bills to punish domestic violence with flogging. Maryland (1882), Delaware (1901), and Oregon (1906) actually passed laws that allowed the use of a whipping post to punish wife beating. However, the punishment was rarely used (Buzawa & Buzawa, 2003; Pleck, 1989).

Feminists considered domestic violence a crime, but were interested in divorce reform legislation that allowed divorce on the grounds of drunkenness or cruelty. They were largely unsuccessful in their attempts to change divorce laws. Over time, feminists gave greater priority to providing resources for victims of domestic violence rather than punishment of perpetrators. Their efforts led to the establishment of a legal aid society for victims of domestic violence, rape, and incest (Pleck, 1989, 2004).

Although not espousing feminist ideology, the women's temperance movement sought to protect women, stabilize the family and enforce morality by forcing men to act responsibly. They considered domestic violence to be an outcome of drinking. The Women's Christian Temperance Union and local women's clubs were influential in providing legal remedies for victims of domestic violence. In an effort to preserve families, the focus turned to rehabilitation of the batterer and reconciliation of the family. However, as rehabilitation gained support, the perception of domestic violence as a serious crime diminished (Pleck, 1989).

By the end of the nineteenth century, the social and political milieu defined domestic violence as a family in crisis, recreating domestic violence as a personal trouble rather than a public issue. The government's role shifted from criminalization of domestic violence to rehabilitation and recreation of family privacy. Reformers developed family courts to reduce and eliminate domestic violence cases from the criminal court docket, providing a specialized forum to deal with families. Policy makers considered the rehabilitative model of intervention (e.g., using social casework methods) to be more humane and appropriate to help what they now considered as dysfunctional families (Buzawa & Buzawa, 2003; Pleck, 1989, 2004). The goal was to keep marriages together at all cost, preserving the batterer's reputation within the community and the husband's responsibility to govern his household (Bevacqua & Baker, 2004). Poverty, poor housing, and genetic inferiority created social problems; domestic violence was an outcome (Pleck, 1989).

Psychoanalytic approaches gained credibility, characterizing domestic violence as a personality flaw or individual pathology rather than a social problem (Pleck, 2004). Family sociologists influenced the practice of family casework, arguing that physical abuse was a manifestation of domestic discord that required treatment in the couple. A valid analysis of the discord required complete understanding of each person's personality and attitude toward the other person in the marriage (Mowrer, 1937). One study characterized battered women as castrating, frigid, aggressive, indecisive, and passive. The battered woman was masochistic and battering met her need for abuse (Snell, Rosenwald, & Robey, 1964). Clinicians were strongly encouraged to take a therapeutic position of neutrality and objectivity toward the client. The battered woman was complicit in her abuse, unable to see that she enabled her husband to batter her through her dependency (Pleck, 2004). Family courts focused on reconciliation rather than criminal behavior. The greater the emphasis on domestic violence as domestic discord, the lower the emphasis on domestic violence as a criminal act (Buzawa & Buzawa, 2003; Pleck, 1989).

As in the 1870s, the definition of domestic violence as personal trouble again shifted to public issue in the latter half of the twentieth century. Increased pressure from victims' advocates, high profile lawsuits, and increases in reporting domestic violence contributed to states implementing strong legislation, enhancing law enforcement responses to domestic violence, and promoting prosecution (Irving, 2002; Woo, 2002; Zorza, 1992). The reforms were much broader and national in scope compared to earlier periods. The first state laws against domestic violence went into effect in 1976, providing funding for shelters, improving reporting procedures, and establishing more effective criminal court proceedings. By 1980, all but six states had implemented such laws (Pleck, 2004).

The 1980s to 1990s saw the emergence of community-focused responses to domestic violence. Developed in Duluth, Minnesota in 1980, the model of a coordinated community response involves developing and implementing policies and procedures that improve coordination of services and leads to uniform responses to domestic violence cases (Shepard, 1999).

The model of a coordinated community response to domestic violence operates under the critical assumption that domestic violence is a public issue rather than personal trouble. Communities, rather than individuals, are responsible for addressing domestic violence by developing policies and procedures to ensure safety for victims while holding batterers accountable. Common components of a coordinated community response include standard policies and procedures for arrest, aggressive prosecution and consistent sentencing, support and advocacy for victims, court mandated battering intervention services for offenders, and monitoring of offender compliance with court orders and terms of probation (Danis, 2003; Shepard, 1999; Shepard, Falk, & Elliot, 2002). While implementation may vary from community to community, overall goals of intervention include provision of safety for the victim, holding offenders accountable, community education, and changing the social systems that support violence (Adler, 2002; Allen, 2006; Post, Klevens, Maxwell, Shelley, & Ingram, 2010; Salazar, Emshoff, Baker, & Crowley, 2007; Shepard, 1999; Shepard et al., 2002; Shepard, 2005).

Texas has followed national trends in its state response to domestic violence. Domestic violence shifted from personal trouble to public issue in Texas when the legislature defined and criminalized family violence in 1979. The Texas Family Code (Section 71.004) defines "Family Violence" as an act by a member of a family or household against another member of the family or household that is intended to result in physical harm, bodily injury, assault or sexual assault or that is a threat that reasonably places the member in fear of imminent physical harm, bodily injury, assault, or sexual assault. It does not include defensive measures to protect oneself.

The county's history of responding to domestic violence parallels national pressures to treat domestic violence as a public issue and as a crime. The response to domestic violence in the county has evolved since advocates established the first battered women's shelter in the area in 1978. Other factors spurred the development of a countywide coordinated community response to domestic violence. For example, alleging that police discriminated against battered women by failing to respond to domestic violence calls and enforce existing laws, battered women filed a class-action lawsuit in 1985 against one of the largest cities in Texas on behalf of all victims of domestic violence. The court ruled in favor of the plaintiffs, underscoring the threat of liability for police inaction. As a result, the ruling acted as a catalyst for system wide changes in law enforcement response and subsequent prosecution in domestic violence cases (Zorza, 1992).

SUMMARY

How a society defines a problem shapes the focus of intervention (Cosimo, 1999; Stone, 2002). Through the doctrine of coverture, domestic violence was defined by the Puritans as "wicked carriage," and considered a sin, a threat to social order, and worthy of punishment. Although largely symbolic, the Massachusetts Bay Colony passed the first law to criminalize domestic violence in the in 1641. Over the next 350 years, the political climate and fluctuating beliefs regarding the privacy of the home and the sanctity of the family influenced the treatment of domestic violence as a personal trouble of milieu or a public issue of social structure (Bailey, 2006; Mills, 1959/2000; Pleck, 1989).

CHAPTER THREE

Criminal Justice Response to Domestic Violence: Theoretical Frameworks

Disciplinary biases within the studies of psychology, sociology, criminology, or within political agendas of activists, unavoidably influence theories of domestic violence (Heise, 1998). However, no single theoretical perspective dominates the field (Michalski, 2005). Based upon the work by Danis (2003), this chapter explores four theoretical frameworks that inform criminal justice responses to domestic violence: social learning, social exchange/deterrence, feminist, and ecological. The chapter briefly describes each theoretical perspective and how it contributes to the community response to domestic violence. For example, social learning theory suggests that violence is learned and can be unlearned, providing the basis for promoting the use of battering intervention programs. Social exchange/deterrence theory provides the framework for issuing protective orders, arrest, prosecution, and sanctions. Feminist theory influenced advocates to frame the issue of domestic violence as a social problem supported by a patriarchal system. Finally, the various levels of the ecological framework integrate social learning theory, social exchange/deterrence theory, and feminist theory into a formalized community response (Danis, 2003).

SOCIAL LEARNING THEORY

From a social learning theoretical perspective, individuals learn through observation and experience. It would be difficult, according to Bandura (1971), to imagine a socialization process that shapes the language, mores, and customs of a culture without the guidance of models who demonstrate cultural mores in their own behavior. Individuals learn through direct observation of role models, indirect or vicarious observation through symbolic modeling, and direct experience (Bandura, 1969, 1973; Davis, Taylor & Maxwell, 2000; Dutton, 1995; Jasinski, 2001). As a result, individuals may learn aggression through three major mediums: the family, the subculture in which the family resides, and symbolic modeling (Bandura, 1969, 1979).

Individuals directly observe behaviors and the consequences of those behaviors through role models provided by parents and significant others. Because individuals have the capacity to learn through observation, they can acquire patterns of behavior without having to form them gradually by trial and error (Bandura, 1969, 1979). The family is a powerful agent of socialization. Goode (1971) notes that parents use force and threats to socialize children, teaching them that force is useful and training them in the use of force and violence. The family as the primary source of socialization models when the use of violence is an appropriate tactic to solve conflicts, and dysfunctional behaviors are passed from one generation to the next (Jasinski, 2001; Portwood & Heany, 2007; Tollefson & Gross, 2006).

Although the family has a major influence in social development of the individual, social networks or subcultures have a major influence on the family. The term *subculture* implies that there are social values that set certain groups apart and prevent integration within the dominant culture (Wolfgang & Ferracuti, 2001). The subculture in which a family resides and with which they have repeated exposure, is an important force in socialization (Bandura, 1979). Cultural norms and values vary among societies, and some may be more accepting of violence as a way of life, as indicated through their socialization processes and within their interpersonal relationships (Bandura, 1979; Payne & Gainey, 2005; Wolfgang & Ferracuti, 2001).

Mass media such as television and film provide symbolic modeling, often portraying violence as the preferred and successful solution to conflict (Bandura, 1979). Bandura contends that symbolic modeling teaches aggressive styles of conduct, alters restraints over aggressive behavior, desensitizes and habituates individuals to violence, and shapes images of reality upon which behaviors are based (Bandura, 1979). Media often portray physical aggression as the preferred and frequently successful solution to conflict. Exposure to violence through the media desensitizes individuals through vicarious observation of repeated acts of violence, rationalizations for committing violence, and demonstrations of violent behaviors (Bandura, 1979; Jasinski, 2001). What is generally lacking from media materials are the consequences for the perpetrator's violent behavior, such as arrest or incarceration (Emmers-Sommer, Pauley, Hanzal, & Triplett, 2006).

However, the social learning theoretical perspective differentiates between the acquisition of destructive behaviors and the factors that determine whether individuals will perform what they have learned. Individuals do not enact everything they learn. While individuals can learn, retain, and have the capability to behave aggressively, they may rarely use violence because it does not have functional value for them or may have negative sanctions. On the other hand, they may engage in violent behaviors, not because they lack self-control but because they have learned to justify morally their violence (Bandura, 1979). Over time, aggressive behaviors are encouraged through past experience, are meaningfully related to the context in which they occur, and are maintained because they serve a purpose for the individual who is enacting them (Toch, 1992). Individuals experience patterns of reinforcement and punishment for aggressive behaviors, learning when their social environment tolerates violence and when violence is ignored (Jasinski, 2001; Hines & Malley-Morrison, 2005). Consequently, violent, aggressive, and abusive behaviors are learned responses that are reinforced through either reward or punishment immediately after the behavior takes place (Bandura, 1973; Bern, 1985; Danis, 2003; Gelles, 1979). Repeated exposure to violence, opportunities for practice in interactions, and rehearsal reinforce aggressive behaviors, which may also have a functional value for persons engaging in violence. Further, individuals with the most power, prestige, and competence tend to be the model for future behavior by the observer (Bandura, 1969, 1973).

SOCIAL EXCHANGE/DETERRENCE THEORY

Community responses to domestic violence rely upon the legal system for deterrence and rest upon the restraining function of punishment. Observed outcomes may reduce the deterrent effects of legal consequences if the chances of arrest and punishment for domestic violence are relatively low (Bandura, 1979). At its most fundamental level, the social exchange theoretical perspective assumes that actions, predicated on rewarding reactions from others, govern social interaction (Blau, 1964; Turner, 1998). The basis of all social processes is the exchange of valued resources (Turner, 1998). Most social exchange theorists restrict the theory to the exchange of positively valued rewards and resources. However, if a reward adds positive value or removes negative value and punishment adds negative value or removes positive value, then both reward and punishment may increase the benefit from the exchange (Molm, 1994). In his early application of social exchange to family violence, Goode (1971) suggested the strongest and most powerful members of the family (usually men and parents) use force, the threat of force, violence, and the threat of violence to gain compliance from those are weakest with the least amount of power. This is demonstrated clearly in domestic violence cases when the cost of being violent does not exceed the reward and constraining social controls are few or nonexistent (Gelles, 1982; Gelles, 1983). When domestic violence is defined as personal trouble that occurs within the private institution of the family, and social institutions are reluctant to consider it as a public issue, the cost of violence is low (Gelles, 1993; Pleck, 1989).

The fear of punishment "gives pause to the evilly inclined" (Durkheim, 1893/1997, p. 44). Deterrence theory suggests a psychological process through which individuals are deterred from committing certain behaviors only if they perceive sanctions will be certain, swift, or severe (Carmody & Williams, 1987; Williams, 2005; Williams & Hawkins, 1986). A negative relationship exists between the perception of sanctions and criminal behavior. As the perception of risk of sanctions for criminal behavior increases, the likelihood that an individual will commit the crime decreases (Piquero & Pogarsky, 2002). Individual personal or vicarious experiences should encourage prevention, reduction, or cessation of violent behaviors. Defining domestic violence as a public issue through societal sanctions increases the cost of violent behavior; individuals will choose alternatives to violent behavior because they fear sanctions that they have experienced either personally or vicariously (Danis, 2003; Williams, 2005).

Deterrence is not a unitary theory, although rational choice constructions of deterrence are widely accepted. Theorists frequently draw a distinction between general deterrence and specific deterrence. General deterrence refers to sanctions experienced vicariously and to the proposition that potential perpetrators consider the cost and benefit of a crime and the sanctions imposed on others (Buzawa & Buzawa, 2003; Carmody & Williams, 1987; Sherman, Smith, Schmidt & Rogan, 1992; Williams, 2005; Williams & Hawkins, 1986). According to general deterrence theory, as the perceived cost of criminal behavior increases, the probability of deterrence increases. This implies the efficacy of the threat of legal sanctions such as statutory penalties, arrest, sentencing, and time incarcerated (Williams & Hawkins, 1986).

Specific deterrence refers to the enforcement of sanctions imposed on an actual perpetrator; threats of future sanctions are more credible and the fear of punishment suppresses further acts of violence (Buzawa & Buzawa, 2003; Sherman et al., 1992; Williams, 2005).

The deterrence theoretical perspective assumes that general deterrence and specific deterrence are distinct types and influence different populations: either punished offenders or the public (Piquero & Paternoster, 1998; Sitren & Applegate, 2007). Stafford and Warr (1993) observe that traditional beliefs about deterrence concentrate on the effects of being punished, ignoring the potential effects of avoiding punishment. They suggest a different approach to deterrence. Their model is a re-conceptualization of general and specific deterrence and proposes that individuals make judgments about the risk of legal sanctions on their behavior based on both personal (direct) and vicarious (indirect) experience of punishment and punishment avoidance. Direct and indirect experiences with punishment increase an individual's perception of the certainty and severity of punishment, and decrease the inclination to offend. In contrast, direct and indirect experiences with punishment avoidance reduce the perception of the certainty of punishment and increase the likelihood of offending (Piquero & Pogarsky, 2002; Sitren & Applegate, 2007; Stafford & Warr, 1993). Contrary to Stafford and Warr's model there appears to be some support for an "emboldening effect," with punishment experiences encouraging rather than deterring future offending (Piquero & Pogarsky, 2002). In general, mixed support for Stafford and Warr's model exists, with only partial support for deterrence (Sitren & Applegate, 2007). This could have implications for direct and indirect deterrence effects when designing community wide interventions for domestic violence cases.

FEMINIST THEORY

In his collection of proverbs first published in 1670, John Ray admonished that: "A spaniel, a woman, and a walnut-tree, the more they're beaten the better still they be" (p. 46) and "A dead wife's the best goods in a man's house" (p. 45). To explore domestic violence from a feminist theoretical perspective, some context is required. A feminist sociology begins with the relations of ruling, according to Smith (1987). The relations of ruling consist of practices organized with an invisible gender subtext, and residing within government, law, business, finance, professional organizations, and educational institutions (Smith, 1987). Largely unexamined and yet institutionalized, the relation of ruling is labeled by Millet (1971) as the birthright of dominance by males, and by Bourdieu (2001) as a masculine sociodicy that gives legitimacy to the relationship of domination by grounding it in a socially constructed biological nature. In the relation of power between men and women, men dominate (Smith, 1987). This relation of dominance is pervasive and provides society with its fundamental concept of power (Millett, 1971). Power, material advantages, and the development of institutions such as theology, philosophy, law, and custom come with masculinity (Fletcher, 1994). The relation of dominance is, at its very core, patriarchal.

What is patriarchy? Weber defines patriarchy as "by far the most important type of domination the legitimacy of which rests upon tradition. Patriarchalism means the authority of the father, the husband, the senior of the house, the sib elder over the members of the household and sib; the rule of the master and patron over bondsmen, serfs, freed men; of the lord over the domestic servants and household officials. . ." (Weber, in Gerth & Mills, 1946, p. 296). Patriarchy is both ideological and structural. Ideologically, patriarchy encompasses beliefs, norms, and values about the status and role of women. The structure of patriarchy determines women's access to resources and positions within social institutions (Yodanis, 2004). However, Fletcher (1994) argues that the structures that support and maintain patriarchy are fluid, adaptable, and adjustable. Men have been shaping and reshaping masculinity for hundreds of years (Fletcher, 1994). Emphasizing social organization, individuals are the product of socialization. Simply, men and women are different because they are socialized differently (Gimenez, 1975).

Gender as power is as much about personal relationships as it is about politics, structures, institutions, and practices (Fletcher, 1994). At the center of a feminist perspective on domestic violence is the key assumption that domestic violence is a complex gendered problem that involves the psychologies of the perpetrator and victim, the role expectations in family relationships, and the society in which the individuals and relationships are embedded (Hines & Malley-Morrison, 2005; Yllö, 1993). Domestic violence is a natural consequence of a socially constructed, institutionally supported patriarchal system. Within the context of this system, men have power over women and, unlike women, have access to material and symbolic resources (Bograd, 1988; Danis, 2003; Dobash & Dobash, 1981; Gimenez, 1975; Vogel, 1983). Strong empirical support exists for the premise that patriarchal norms and structural inequality correlate to some extent to male violence against women (Hines & Malley-Morrison, 2005; Michalski, 2004; Yllö, 1993; Yodanis, 2004). Although social class and racial differences exist, all men can potentially use violence or the threat of violence as a powerful means to subordinate women. Violence is the most overt and effective method of maintaining social control (Bograd, 1988). Even if individual men do not use physical violence or threats of violence against their intimate partners, men as a class benefit as women curtail life activities because of their fear of violence by their male partners or strangers. The reality of domination at the social level contributes to and maintains domestic violence at the personal level (Bograd, 1988; Edelson & Tolman, 1992).

Battered women's advocates have been highly successful in their efforts to criminalize domestic violence, resulting in mandatory arrest policies, protective orders, and specialized domestic violence courts (Buzawa & Buzawa, 2003; Danis, 2003; Shepard, 2005). However, those who consider domestic violence to be rooted in patriarchal norms and structures have been concerned that the state's response to domestic violence would recreate rather than ameliorate patriarchal culture in the home and in the government (Mirchandani, 2006). Historically, court involvement focused on preservation of the family rather than the health and welfare of the battered woman (Pleck, 1989; 2004). In her review of a domestic violence court in Salt Lake City, Mirchandani (2006) suggested that courts might incorporate ideas about patriarchal genesis of domestic violence and confront male dominance and control through holding batterers responsible for their violence. Acting upon the premise that domestic violence is rooted in patriarchal norms and social structures, some communities design strategies to educate men on how patriarchal systems socialize and inform males (Douglas, Bathrick, & Perry, 2008).

ECOLOGICAL FRAMEWORK

An ecological framework approaches domestic violence as a multifaceted phenomenon grounded in the interaction among personal, situational, and sociocultural factors (Heise, 1998). The framework integrates social and psychological characteristics, analyzing human development and behavior through a nested set of environmental contexts, each contained within the next (Bronfenbrenner, 1977). These successive levels are labeled ontogenic development, the microsystem, mesosystem, exosystem, macrosystem, and the chronosystem (Belsky, 1980; Bronfenbrenner, 1977, 1986; Dutton, 1995; Heise, 1998; Malley-Morrison & Hines, 2004). The strength of the ecological framework is that it considers what takes place within the context of the family, the forces at work in the larger social system in which the family resides, and the cultural beliefs and values that influence the family and the social system (Belsky, 1980). Applied to the specific phenomenon of domestic violence, a series of systems interact to affect the development and maintenance of violent behaviors (Edelson & Tolman, 1992).

Ontogenic development refers to the personal history factors that may influence an individual's behavior and relationships with others (Belsky, 1980; Dutton, 1995; Heise, 1998). These features of a person's developmental experience may shape his or her response to the family setting and the role within the family (Belsky, 1980). For men who are violent with their intimate partners, only two developmental experiences have emerged as risk factors for future abusive behaviors:

witnessing domestic violence as a child, and experiencing physical or sexual abuse as a child (Heise, 1998).

The microsystem level refers to the relations between the person and environment in an immediate setting containing that person. The setting may be the home, neighborhood, church, workplace, or another environment in which participants interact according to specific roles, such as daughter, parent, husband, or wife (Bronfenbrenner, 1977; Edleson & Tolman, 1992). For men who are violent with their intimate partners, the microsystem reflects the immediate context in which the abuse takes place (Dutton, 1995; Edelson & Tolman, 1992; Heise, 1998). Microsystemic factors related to increased risk of perpetrating domestic violence include male dominance over economic and decision-making authority in the family, marital conflict, and to some extent, heavy alcohol consumption (Heise, 1998).

The mesosystem level refers to the interrelations among major setting which influence and link the microsystems in a person's social environment (Bronfenbrenner, 1977, 1986; Edelson & Tolman, 1992). These interrelations include those between the family and the extended family, peers, place of work, and place of worship. They may also include linkages between the family and social institutions such as the police, courts, and social services (Edelson & Tolman, 1992).

The exosystem is an extension of the mesosystem and refers to the formal and informal social structures that affect the immediate setting in which the person is situated, and may influence, delimit, or even determine what happens in the setting. Social structures encompass but are not limited to work, neighborhood, mass media, governments, and the distribution of goods and services (Bronfenbrenner, 1977; Edelson & Tolman, 1992). The exosystem also includes interactions engaged in by others, such as police, prosecutors, probation officers, and social workers that could have an impact on an individual's behaviors and thinking (Edelson & Tolman, 1992). Exosystem factors linked to domestic violence include unemployment, low socioeconomic status, and social isolation (Heise, 1998).

The macrosystem is fundamentally different from the other systems in that it does not refer to specific contexts affecting the life of an individual. It refers to the overarching institutional rules, patterns, values, and beliefs of the culture or subculture. It includes the economic, social, educational, legal, and political systems, and its influence is evident in the microsystems, macrosystems, and exosystems (Bronfenbrenner, 1977; Dutton, 1995; Edelson & Tolman, 1992). For example, one of the most stable macrosystemic factors that promote violence toward women is a cultural definition of masculinity linked to dominance, toughness, or male honor (Heise, 1998). Other factors may include adherence to rigid gender roles, a sense of male entitlement or ownership over women, approval of physical chastisement of women under certain circumstances, and condoning violence as a way to resolve conflict (Beesley & McGuire, 2009; Heise, 1998; Lawson, Brossart , & Shefferman, 2010).

Although Bronfenbrenner (1986) describes the chronosystem as the impact of life transitions throughout the life span, Edelson and Tolman (1992) extend the chronosystem to include all histories within the ecological framework. To that end, their perspective of the chronosystem encompasses the history of cultural attitudes toward violence and male-female relationships.

In summary, the ecological framework begins with the individual man, with his personal history (ontogenic development), in direct interactions with others within varied settings that form microsystems. The network of microsystems forms the man's mesosystem. Others within his network of microsystems engage in relationships in additional settings in which he is not directly involved, creating exosystems within his ecology that have an impact on him. Even more removed are the cultural values and beliefs that form his macrosystem and influence his interactions with others. Holding all systems together is the chronosystem, the historical underpinning that reflects the depth of time and its effect on all systems (Edelson & Tolman, 1992).

LEGAL SANCTIONS FOR DOMESTIC VIOLENCE

As noted in Chapter One, for the purposes of this study, "legal sanctions" are defined as activities that are carried out in a community in response to domestic violence offenses and that include civil protective orders, arrest, probation, revocation of probation, and incarceration. The justice system typically generates legal sanctions are typically generated through the justice system, which has both a symbolic and a real role in community responses to domestic violence (Dobash, 2003). It is symbolic in the sense that the justice system deems what is right, what is wrong, and what a civilized society will tolerate. Through symbolic modeling, society learns what really counts as justice particularly if social controls are few and the perceived cost of violence is low (Bandura, 1979; Dobash, 2003; Gelles, 1993; Pleck, 1989). In another sense, the role of the justice system is real and pragmatic in terms of direct responses to persons who commit violence and their victims. The justice system response may indicate either that domestic violence is of little importance or, conversely, that domestic violence is unacceptable and warrants concerted action (Dobash, 2003).

One approach to a community response to domestic violence is through a perspective of justice as fairness, that all citizens are free and equal and that victims of domestic violence have the moral power to take part in society as equal citizens, including freedom from unjust personal harm (Logan, Shannon, Walker, & Faragher, 2006; Rawls & Kelly, 2001). The fundamental purpose of the community response is to reduce, if not eliminate, harm. To that end, community responses to domestic violence include sanctions addressed through the legal system in two distinct ways: the civil protective orders and the criminal justice process.

Civil Protective Orders

The civil process includes but is not limited to divorce, lawsuits for damages caused by domestic violence, and protective orders (Buzawa & Buzawa, 2003; Logan, Shannon, Walker, & Faragher, 2006; Logan & Walker, 2010). Prior to 1972, the only civil remedy available to a victim of domestic violence was an injunction against the abuser during the process of legal separation or divorce (Buzawa & Buzawa, 2003; Zorza, 1992). There were limitations to the orders, however. The victim had to be married to the abuser and the injunctions were available in only a few states. They typically expired within a very short time. If the abuser violated the injunction, there were no criminal penalties for the violation (Zorza, 1992). By 1994, all fifty states and the District of Columbia enacted laws that permitted victims of domestic violence to petition the court for a civil protective order and authorized civil courts to issue protective orders against current and former intimate partners (Carlson, Harris, & Holden, 1999; Irving, 2002; Morao, 2006; Rousseve, 2005; Woo, 2002).

Protective orders are binding civil court orders, developed to provide some measure of protection for victims of domestic violence (Logan, Shannon, Walker, & Faragher, 2006; Logan & Walker, 2010). Civil protective orders prohibit the person found to have committed domestic violence from committing further domestic violence, communicating directly to the person protected by the order in a threatening or harassing manner, making threats, and going to or near the residence, or place of employment of a person protected by the order, or a member of the family or household of the person protected by the order. This also includes any conduct that is likely to harass, annoy, alarm, abuse, torment, or embarrass the person. Violation of a protective order may result in limited criminal penalties such as a small fine, short imprisonment, or both (Carlson, Harris, & Holden, 1999; Morao, 2006; Texas Family Code, Chapter 85; Rousseve, 2005). Because protective orders are not criminal cases, the civil rules of procedure apply. The evidentiary standard is a preponderance of evidence that domestic violence has occurred, which is a lower burden of proof than the standard of beyond reasonable doubt required in criminal cases (Buzawa & Buzawa, 2003; Logan & Walker, 2010). A victim may be more willing to apply for a protective order with the belief that there is less chance of retaliation than with criminal proceedings (Carlson, Harris, & Holden, 1999).

In their study of protective order effectiveness, Logan and Walker (2010) found that there were significant reductions in abuse and violence during the course of the 6-month follow-up period. However, Logan and Walker also found that stalking was a significant risk factor for protective order violations. Other researchers have found that the effectiveness of protective orders appears closely related to how specific the orders are and how well they are enforced (Keilitz, Davis, Efkeman, Flango, & Hannaford, 1998). From a deterrence perspective, the penalties associated with violation of the order may act as a deterrent to further violence (Carlson, Harris, & Holden, 1999). For example, in Travis County, Texas, researchers concluded that there was merit to protective orders as one tool to reduce domestic violence. They found a 66% decrease in police contacts, comparing two years prior to two years post protective order (Carlson, Harris, and Holden, 1999). However, the failure of police to enforce protective orders in some communities implies that abusers can violate the order with impunity (Morao, 2006; Zorza, 1992). Non-prosecuted cases of protective order violations against victims tended to have higher rates of revictimization when compared to cases where violations were prosecuted (Wooldredge & Thistlethwaite, 2005).

Typically, research on recidivism of domestic violence has focused on the criminal courts and protective orders, or "stay away" orders imposed by criminal courts as part of sentencing (Bouffard & Muftić, 2007; Cissner & Puffett, 2006; Klein & Crowe, 2008; Labriola, Rempel, & Davis, 2005; Murphy, Musser, & Maton, 1998). None of these studies on recidivism examined civil protective orders as a sanction for domestic violence related offenses. Prior research on civil protective orders has focused on examining the civil protective order as the sole sanction imposed for domestic violence (Carlson, Harris, and Holden, 1999; Logan et al., 2006; Mears, Carlson, Holden & Harris, 2001), the presence of a protective order at the time of arrest for domestic violence (Kingsnorth, 2006), and recidivism of offenders who were under a civil protective order (Etter & Birzer, 2007). Examining the effects of protective orders, arrest, and the combination of protective order and arrest in reducing the prevalence or time to revictimization for victims of domestic violence, Mears et al. (2001) found that no one intervention was more effective than another. With the exception of Mears et al. (2001), there have been no studies that include civil protective orders as one of a number of legal sanctions imposed for a single case, as examined by this study.

Criminal Justice Responses

The second way to address domestic violence through the legal system is to arrest and prosecute the individual accused of perpetrating domestic violence through the criminal courts. If convicted, the court may then mandate participation in a range of options including but not limited to fines, incarceration, probation, and completion of a battering intervention program (Bouffard & Muftić, 2007; Buzawa & Buzawa, 2003; Danis, 2003; Davis, Taylor, & Maxwell, 2000; Gondolf, 2002; Kingsnorth, 2006; Klein, 2008; Shepard & Pence, 1999).

<u>Arrest</u>
After almost 20 years of research on arrest as a deterrent promoting the reduction, cessation, or prevention of domestic violence, the efficacy of

arrest remains an open question (Danis, 2003; Maxwell, Garner, & Fagan, 2001; Williams, 2005). The most influential studies on this issue were six field experiments conducted between 1981 and 1991 by six police departments and research teams (Maxwell, Garner, & Fagan, 2001). Researchers conducted the original study in Minneapolis. To replicate the original study, the National Institute of Justice funded the remaining five field experiments, otherwise referred to as the Spouse Assault Replication Program (SARP). Researchers designed the experiments to test the notion that arrests reduced recidivism better than less formal alternatives such as crisis intervention or mediation (Berk & Newton, 1985; Buzawa & Buzawa, 2003; Maxwell, Garner, & Fagan, 2001; Sherman & Berk, 1984).

Sherman and Berk (1984) conducted the original study, which took place in Minneapolis in 1981 and 1982. Police faced three different and conflicting options when called to a domestic violence scene: forced separation of the couple to achieve short-term peace, mediation to get to the underlying cause of the dispute, or arrest. The options were a fundamental component of the research design, which called for random assignment of arrest, separation, or some form of advice, which could include mediation. The design only applied to misdemeanor assaults where both victim and suspect were present. Exceptions to the random assignment were cases where the batterer attempted to assault the officers, the victim demanded arrest, or both people were injured. There were no exceptions, however, regarding the sex of the suspect or victim. The researchers conducted 205 interviews out of the full sample of 314 victims and found that among these 205 cases, 83% of the suspects were males who either were or had been intimate partners with their victims. The remaining suspects were sons, brothers, roommates, or others (15%) followed by wives or girlfriends (2%) (Sherman & Berk, 1984). Researchers did a six-month follow-up to determine if the batterer committed a repeat assault, destroyed property, or threatened assault. The results suggested that, unlike separation or advice, arrest and initial incarceration produced a deterrent effect and contributed to the deterrence potential of the criminal justice system. However, Sherman and Berk cautioned against instituting mandatory arrest policies, favoring some police discretion.

The multisite SARP of the Minneapolis experiment allowed each of the five sites to vary the eligibility criteria for inclusion in study. For example, one site included only married couples; another site included same-sex couples and siblings (Maxwell, Garner, & Fagan, 2001). The five SARP sites completed their experiments and produced mixed results (Maxwell, Garner, & Fagan, 2001; Sherman, Smith, Schmidt, & Rogan, 1992). The results from three studies indicated no long-term deterrent effects of arrest on subsequent assaults. In fact, the data suggested significant long-term increases in repeat assaults. The remaining two SARP experiments supported the findings in Minneapolis with evidence of long-term deterrent effects, but with no escalation effects (Berk, Campbell, Klap, & Western, 1992; Maxwell, Garner, & Fagan, 2001; Sherman, Smith, Schmidt, & Rogan, 1992). However, a multisite pooled analysis of the five replication experiments, which included only cases with a male suspect and a female victim, found evidence of a consistent, direct, and modest deterrent effect of arrest, reducing repeat assaults. The analysis also indicated that arrest had no effect on a minority of batterers who continued to commit domestic violence. Finally, a majority of batterers stopped their aggressive behaviors even without arrest. The deterrent effects of arrest were consistent but modest when compared with the overall percentage of batterers who desisted from committing domestic violence (Maxwell, Garner, & Fagan, 2001).

Despite Sherman and Berk's caution against mandatory arrest as a policy, many states and the District of Columbia have enacted laws mandating arrest in domestic violence cases. If a community chooses to implement a mandatory or preferred arrest policy for domestic violence, police officers must be empowered to make arrests in when the officer has probable cause to believe that an individual committed domestic violence (Rousseve, 2005). This is possible with warrantless arrests. Warrantless arrests are a deviation from the general rule that police officers may not make an arrest for misdemeanor assault unless the assault occurs in the officers' presence (Irving, 2002; Zorza, 1992). Currently, all 50 states and the District of Columbia permit warrantless arrests in domestic violence cases (Irving, 2002; Woo, 2002). The state of Texas allows warrantless arrests when the officer has probable cause to believe that an individual committed an offense involving domestic violence, or violated a protective order (Frost, 2006; Texas Code of Criminal Procedure). Though the single act of arrest has generated inordinate amounts of attention from researchers and policy makers, the intervention of arrest is simply not enough. Criminal justice responses must deal with the violence that gave rise to the arrest, or the intervention is likely to be ineffective and repeat offenses are to be expected (Dobash, 2003).

Prosecution and Case Disposition

A number of options are available to the courts in dealing with domestic violence cases, including non-prosecution or dismissal of the case by the judge. If the case moves forward and the defendant is convicted, sentencing options include jail, probation, mandated participation in a battering intervention program, or any combination thereof (Davis, Smith, & Nickles, 1998). Research suggests that prosecution and resulting dispositions that consider a defendant's risk to reoffend can significantly deter recidivism of domestic violence assault (Klein, 2008). Some jurisdictions have adopted "no-drop" prosecution policies, with the intent to increase offender accountability and curb prosecutorial discretion. Under such policies, prosecutors may not drop domestic violence charges at the victim's request. Instead, they must pursue the charges and proceed with or without the victim's testimony or cooperation (Morao, 2006; Rousseve, 2005). One study found that cases processed in a jurisdiction that mandated prosecution increased the prevalence and duration of case processing and court oversight but a lower probability of conviction. However, the researchers argue, the longer case processing time for jurisdictions with mandatory prosecution is not necessarily a sign of inefficiency because the batterer is monitored by the court prior to trial (Peterson & Dixon, 2005).

Researchers have found mixed results on the deterrent effects of prosecution, however. For example, Davis, Smith, and Nickles (1998) found no evidence that prosecution outcomes affected recidivism, suggesting that prosecution may not have a deterrent effect. Murphy, Musser, and Maton (1998) found that case outcome was not significantly associated with recidivism, although individuals who received a guilty verdict or probation had lower recidivism rates. In contrast, Ventura and Davis (2004) found that domestic violence convictions had a moderate deterrent effect on domestic violence recidivism; however, the deterrent value tended to weaken when the sanction was a suspended sentence without probation, or if the sanction was a fine. Wooldredge (2007) found evidence that full prosecution with conviction reduced the odds of committing another domestic violence assault. Other research suggests that the severity of the sentence, rather than the length of the sentence, may contribute to reducing recidivism of domestic violence for persons arrested and charged with misdemeanor assault (Thistlethwaite, Wooldredge, & Gibbs, 1998).

The dispositions of cases for persons who commit domestic violence vary widely, although most jurisdictions prosecute these cases as misdemeanor assaults (Klein, 2008). The typical disposition for misdemeanor assault cases is probation. If the court imposes a jail term, it tends to be of short duration (Buzawa & Buzawa, 2003). When comparing case disposition of domestic violence offenders placed on probation to those placed on probation for other violent offenses, researchers found that persons placed on probation for domestic violence offenses were more likely to be required to pay a fine and be court ordered to some type of intervention program. Domestic violence offenders were three times more likely to revictimize their original victim. Their findings also suggest that domestic violence offenders are very similar to other violent offenders in terms of their behavior, compliance with probation, and criminal histories (Olson & Stalans, 2001).

BATTERING INTERVENTION AND PREVENTION PROGRAMS

Referral to a battering intervention program is another case disposition option for domestic violence offenders. In a survey of 260 communities, researchers found that courts most often imposed battering intervention program mandates on convicted offenders originally charged with misdemeanor assaults. In addition to battering intervention program, courts also mandated to other types of programs such as alcohol and substance abuse treatment, mental health services, and anger management (Labriola, Rempel et al., 2007; Labriola, Bradley, et al., 2009).

Battering intervention programs emerged during the mid 1970's using consciousness-raising techniques reframing violence towards an intimate partner as a pattern of controlling behaviors rather than impulsive or uncontrolled acts of violence (Gondolf, 2002; Hamby,

1998; Mederos, 1999). Beginning in Duluth, Minnesota in 1980, battering intervention groups became an integral component of a community wide system approach to domestic violence, which included sanctions such as civil protective orders, arrest, prosecution, and sentencing (Shepard & Pence, 1999).

Battering intervention programs operate under the premise that batterers can change their abusive behaviors (Buzawa & Buzawa, 2003). Intervention programs tend to draw upon several theoretical perspectives. The first theoretical perspective includes family systems, which attributes violence to social learning and the ecological framework. The second theoretical perspective considers individual based theories, which attribute violence to psychological disorders, motivations, or childhood experiences, as in the ontogenic development within the ecological framework. Finally, battering intervention programs draw upon societal and cultural theories such as social exchange and deterrence and the feminist theoretical perspective, which attribute domestic violence to social structures (Healey, Smith, & O'Sullivan, 1998).

Harkening back to the practice of family casework in the early twentieth century, the family systems model approaches domestic violence as a symptom of dysfunction within the family; each member of the family contributes equally to the problem. From a family systems perspective, the interaction produces the violence. No one person is responsible for the violence because the interaction is the problem, not the pathology of one person. The focus of intervention is solving the problem rather than looking for causes. The process puts emphasis on positive interactions, examining times when the couple has not been violent (Healey, Smith, & O'Sullivan, 1998). Critics of the family systems approach to battering intervention note that treating domestic violence as a problem shared by the couple denies the perpetrator's responsibility for his violence, implies blame for the victim, and obscures the seriousness of the act. Ethically, it could be dangerous to counsel victims and batterers together. Encouraging the victim to discuss sensitive issues in the presence of her batterer, including the violence perpetrated against her by the batterer, can put her at risk for further violence once the session is over (Gondolf, 2002; Hansen, 1993; Healey, Smith, & O'Sullivan, 1998). Courts have the authority to sentence the offender, but not the victim, to intervention. To address personal accountability for domestic violence, most state standards and guidelines for court ordered battering intervention programs prohibit interventions that include victim participation, such as couples or family counseling (Babcock, Green, & Robie, 2004; Gondolf, 2002; Healey, Smith, & O'Sullivan, 1998). Two models of battering intervention focus on the individual functioning and psychological motivations of the batterer. The first is the psychodynamic approach. Psychodynamic approaches attend to the emotional composition and personality of the batterer. Uncovering unconscious problems and solving them consciously is a primary tenet of psychodynamic counseling. For example, according to this model, men may have unresolved concerns surrounding their upbringing and personal victimization, which could result in emotional pain, poor impulse control, intimacy, or attachment issues. The goal of counseling is to expose and resolve the underlying cause of the violent behavior (Gondolf, 2002; Healey, Smith, & O'Sullivan, 1998). The second model is cognitive-behavioral therapy. Cognitive-behavioral battering intervention approaches expose patterns of thought (or cognitions) that justify and support the violent behaviors. An underlying premise is violence serves a function for the batterer; violence forces victim compliance and gives a sense of power and control over the situation. As a result, men who batter learn that violence is rewarding because it gives them what they want. Because violence is a learned behavior, from a cognitive behavioral perspective, men who batter can learn non-violence. In addition, cognitive-behavioral models incorporate skills such as communication, conflict resolution, assertiveness, and stress reduction into the counseling to identify and promote awareness of alternative and more acceptable behaviors than violence (Babcock, Green, & Robie, 2004; Gondolf, 2002; Healey, Smith, & O'Sullivan, 1998). Critics of the cognitive-behavioral approach contend that it fails to explain why men credited with dysfunctional thought patterns or skills deficits are frequently not violent in other relationships (Healey, Smith, & O'Sullivan, 1998).

A prominent model used in battering intervention is the Duluth model (Kernsmith & Kernsmith, 2009). Developed in Minnesota by the Duluth Domestic Abuse Intervention Project (DAIP) in 1984, the Duluth model curriculum is what Gondolf terms a "gender-based cognitive-behavioral approach" (Gondolf, 2002, p. 12) and Babcock et al. (2004) consider to be a feminist psycho-educational approach. Based on the theory that violence is functional and used to control people's behavior, DAIP designed the curriculum for use within a community response to domestic violence, which also includes law enforcement, the civil and criminal court system, probation, and counseling agencies. According to this model, men who batter are socialized into a culture that supports and justifies relationships of dominance, with cultural norms and values that implicitly or explicitly tolerate the use of violence against women. Using consciousness-raising exercises, the model challenges personal beliefs about sexism, male privilege, and male socialization. The model considers violence to be a pattern of behaviors rather than discrete episodes of violent behaviors. To change patterns of behavior, men must acknowledge the destructiveness of their violent behaviors, accept responsibility, and focus on nonviolent behaviors and equality in relationships (Babcock, Green, & Robie, 2004; Gondolf, 2002; Healey, Smith, & O'Sullivan, 1998; Pence & Paymar, 1993). Critics of the Duluth model claim that it overemphasizes societal and cultural factors to the exclusion of individual factors, such as childhood abuse and witnessing domestic violence as a child (Healey, Smith, & O'Sullivan, 1998).

The influence of battering intervention programs on the cessation of domestic violence has been controversial. At least four controlled experimental studies have been completed (Bennett et al., 2007), and over 50 quasi-experimental and non-experimental evaluation studies of battering intervention programs have been conducted. While the results are inconclusive, the findings suggest that battering intervention programs have some effects on recidivism of domestic violence (Bennett et al., 2007; Gondolf, 2004; Klein, 2008). Modest effect sizes are attributed to, among other things, unidentified and untreated substance abuse and mental disorders (Jones, D'Agostino, Gondolf, & Heckert, 2004; Tollefson & Gross, 2006), "stake in conformity" issues (Feder & Dugan, 2002; Klein & Crowe, 2008; Sherman, Smith, Schmidt, & Rogan, 1992; Thistlethwaite, Wooldredge, & Gibbs, 1998), inclusion of those who have been generally violent in programs that are not designed for general antisocial behavior (Boyle, O'Leary, Rosenbaum, & Hassett-Walker, 2008; Jewell & Wormith, 2010; Olver, Stockdale, & Wormith, 2011), and applying individual interventions to a social level problem (Bennett et al., 2007). Another reason for the modest effect size of battering intervention programs is a relatively high participant attrition rate, ranging from 25 percent to 89 percent (Bennett et al., 2007; Klein, 2008). Despite program limitations, research suggests that men who complete a battering intervention program are less likely to be rearrested or have a protective order filed against them in the future than those who drop-out of a program or simply do not attend (Babcock, Green, & Robie, 2004; Bennett et al., 2007; Gondolf, 2002; Gordon & Moriarty, 2003; Taylor, Davis, & Maxwell, 2001).

Domestic violence cases are complicated. Although the criminal justice system has a role to play in protecting victims from abuse, it may not be the decisive factor in stopping domestic violence (Davis, Smith, & Nickles, 1998; Davis, Taylor & Maxwell, 2000; Klein & Tobin, 2008). In their 10-year longitudinal study following 342 men arrested for domestic violence related offenses, Klein and Tobin (2008) found that most of the men in their sample did not experience re-arrest for domestic violence or any other crime during the first year, suggesting that the court dispositions acted as a deterrent. However, the suppression effects were short-term. Nine years after the initial arrest for domestic violence, 71% of the men in the sample either were arrested for new crimes or were brought to civil court for new abuse during the follow-up period. However, the researchers found that probation supervision of domestic violence offenders significantly reduces recidivism for among offenders who had few prior criminal offenses, compared to offenders with more substantial criminal histories (Klein & Tobin, 2008).

RISK FACTORS FOR RECIDIVISM

Risk factors are individual characteristics that could increase the likelihood of recidivism, but are not necessarily causal (Gondolf, 2002). Prior research identifies a number of risk factors for recidivism of domestic violence. These include being younger at the time of arrest for the index case (Hanson, Wallace-Capretta, 2004; Johnson, 2008; MacLeod et al., 2009; Ventura & Davis, 2005), prior criminal history for domestic violence assault (Bouffard & Muftić, 2007; Feder & Dugan, 2002; Johnson, 2008; MacLeod et al., 2009; Ventura & Davis, 2005), and prior criminal history for non-domestic violence offenses (Bouffard & Muftić, 2007; Gondolf, 2002; Klein & Crowe, 2008; Klein

& Tobin, 2008; MacLeod et al., 2009). Other risk factors include alcohol or substance abuse (Gondolf, 2002; Hanson & Wallace-Capretta, 2004; Hirschel, Hutchison, & Shaw, 2010; Tollefson & Gross, 2006), employment instability (Johnson, 2008), and psychological disorders (Gondolf, 2002; Tollefson & Gross, 2006). The extent of a person's social bonding to their community, otherwise referred to as a "stake in conformity," is another risk factor for domestic violence recidivism (Sherman et al., 1992). For example, as measures of stake in conformity, Feder and Dugan (2002) considered such variables such as employment, home ownership, length of county and city residency, income, and marital status. They found that offenders with greater stakes in conformity have more to lose from arrest or incarceration and are more likely to be compliant with legal sanctions. One of the limitations of this particular study is that data related to risk factors of recidivism are limited to age, prior court involvement for domestic violence, and prior court involvement for non-domestic violence offenses. The data do not include individual characteristics such as alcohol or substance abuse, employment stability, psychological disorders, or measures of stake in conformity (Feder & Dugan, 2002).

RESEARCH QUESTIONS AND HYPOTHESES

This section presents each hypothesis, the rationale for each hypothesis, and the research question answered by the analyses. Hypotheses 1 relates to demographic variables (age and race/ethnicity). Hypotheses 2 is concerned with prior civil court involvement for protective orders and criminal court involvement for domestic violence related and non-domestic violence related offenses. Hypothesis 3 examines the relative risk of recidivism and cumulative legal sanction variables, as measured by the Legal Sanction Dose-Response Index. Hypothesis 4 concerns the relative risk of recidivism and completion in a court ordered battering intervention program. Finally, Hypothesis 5 examines the hazard of recidivism and time spent incarcerated during the follow-up period.

Demographics and Recidivism

Hypothesis 1a.
The hazard ratio for recidivism for domestic violence related offenses is negatively related to age at the time of the index case offense. Prior

research demonstrates that age, particular a younger age, is a risk factor for recidivism of domestic violence (Hanson, Wallace-Capretta, 2004; Johnson, 2008; MacLeod et al., 2009; Ventura & Davis, 2005). As a risk factor, does age influence how long a man maintains his non-recidivism status?

Hypothesis 1b
The relative risk of recidivism for domestic violence related offenses is not associated with race or ethnicity. Some researchers have found that race and/or ethnicity is not a risk factor for recidivism (Murphy, Musser, and Maton, 1998; Shepard, Falk, & Elliott, 2002; Ventura & Davis, 2005). Does race or ethnicity influence how long a man maintains his non-recidivism status?

Prior Court Involvement and Recidivism

Hypothesis 2a
The relative risk of recidivism for domestic violence related offenses is greater for men with prior civil court involvement for protective orders than for men with no prior civil court involvement for protective orders. Social learning theory proposes that individuals learn through direct experience. Violent behaviors are learned behaviors; they are meaningful within their context and reinforced through either reward or punishment immediately after the behavior has taken place (Bandura, 1973; Bern, 1985; Danis, 2003; Gelles, 1979; Toch, 1992). In social exchange theory, the cost of the violent behavior does not exceed the rewards and constraining social controls are few (Gelles, 1982; Gelles, 1983). A civil protective order is the sanction with the least constraint. It is not a criminal case, but violation of a civil protective order may result in limited criminal penalties (Carlson, Harris, & Holden, 1999; Morao, 2006; Texas Family Code, Chapter 85; Rousseve, 2005). As the least constraining legal sanction, does prior civil court involvement for protective orders influence how long a man maintains his non-recidivism status?

Hypothesis 2b
The relative risk of recidivism for domestic violence related offenses is greater for men with prior criminal court involvement for domestic

violence related offenses than for men with no prior criminal court involvement for domestic violence related offenses. Prior research indicates that prior criminal court involvement for domestic violence is a risk factor for recidivism (Bouffard & Muftić, 2007; Feder & Dugan, 2002; Johnson, 2008; MacLeod et al., 2009; Ventura & Davis, 2005). Does prior criminal court involvement for domestic violence related offenses influence how long a man maintains non-recidivism status?

Hypothesis 2c
The relative risk of recidivism for domestic violence related offenses is greater for men with prior criminal court involvement for non-domestic violence related offenses than for men with no prior criminal court involvement for non-domestic violence related offenses. Prior research suggests that the risk of recidivism is greater for men with a history of involvement with the criminal courts (Bouffard & Muftić, 2007; Gondolf, 2002; Klein & Crowe, 2008; Klein & Tobin, 2008; MacLeod et al., 2009). Does prior criminal court involvement influence how long a man maintains his non-recidivism status?

Legal Sanctions Dose- Response Index and Recidivism

Hypothesis 3
The hazard ratio for recidivism of domestic violence is greater for men with fewer legal sanctions for the index case, as measured by the Legal Sanctions Dose- Response Index. According to deterrence theory, personal and vicarious experience of sanctions should increase perception of the certainty and severity of punishment for domestic violence offenses and decrease recidivism (Piquero & Pogarsky, 2002; Sitren & Applegate, 2007; Stafford & Warr, 1993). For the purposes of this research, dose-responses include any civil protective order, arrest, probation, revocation, and incarceration applied as legal sanctions for the index case. Does the number of sanctions imposed for the index case influence how long a man maintains his non-recidivism status?

Battering Intervention Program Participation and Recidivism

Hypothesis 4
The relative risk of recidivism for domestic violence related offenses is greater for men who did not complete a court-ordered battering

intervention program than for men who completed a court-ordered battering intervention program. From a feminist theoretical perspective, domestic violence is rooted in patriarchal norms and structural inequality and is the most overt and effective means of maintaining social control (Bograd, 1988; Hines & Malley-Morrison, 2005; Michalski, 2004; Yllö, 1993; Yodanis, 2004). Based on the theory that violence is functional, learned, and used to control others, battering intervention programs create an environment in which men may acknowledge the destructiveness of their violent behaviors, accept responsibility, and focus on respectful, nonviolent behaviors and equality in relationships (Babcock, Green, & Robie, 2004; Gondolf, 2002; Healey, Smith, & O'Sullivan, 1998; Pence & Paymar, 1993). Does completion of a battering intervention influence how long a man maintains his non-recidivism status?

Opportunity and Recidivism

Hypothesis 5
The hazard of recidivism for domestic violence related offenses is negatively associated with the length of periods of incarceration for any criminal offenses committed after the index case. As noted by Tollefson and Gross (2006), including individuals in the analyses who did not have the opportunity to reoffend would artificially lower the recidivism rate. This study addresses the issue of opportunity to recidivate through the Cox proportional hazards regression model because it censors those who do not reoffend and does not consider them in the analysis. Because incarceration reduces opportunities for recidivism, does incarceration after the index case influence how long a man maintains his non-recidivism status?

SUMMARY

While no single theoretical perspective dominates the field, Danis (2003) identified four theoretical frameworks that inform criminal justice system responses to domestic violence: social learning theory, social exchange/deterrence theory, feminist theory, and the ecological framework. Social learning theory suggests that behaviors are learned responses reinforced through either reward or punishment (Bandura,

1973). Social exchange/deterrence theory assumes that the reactions of others predicate social interaction (Blau, 1864; Turner, 1998). However, individuals are deterred from committing certain behaviors only if they perceive that the reaction to their behavior is in the form of certain, swift, or severe sanctions (Cormody & Williams, 1987; Williams, 2005; Williams & Hawkins, 1986). According to feminist theory, domestic violence is a natural consequence of a socially constructed, institutionally supported patriarchal society (Bograd, 1988). The fourth theoretical perspective, the ecological framework, considers the context of domestic violence within the family and the community (Belsky, 1980). These theories provide a background against which each community responds to domestic violence, creating and enforcing sanctions such as civil protection orders, arrest, prosecution, and disposition of cases.

CHAPTER FOUR

Research Methods and Data

How long were the men in the sample able to refrain from domestic violence after the index case which brought them to the attention of the civil or criminal courts and resulted in court orders to attend battering intervention programs? After the imposition of legal sanctions, how and to what extent are age, race/ethnicity, prior civil and criminal involvement with the courts, court involvement for the index case, battering intervention program completion, and time incarcerated for offenses other than the index case associated with recidivism of domestic violence? This chapter explains the rationale for this study, and describes the research design, data sources, sampling frame, dependent and independent variables, hypotheses, and analysis. Finally, the chapter discusses the limitations of the data and methods used for this research.

RESEARCH DESIGN

The purpose of this research is to determine the impact of legal sanctions upon the recidivism of men who committed domestic violence in a selected county in Texas and who were court ordered to attend a battering intervention program. This research uses a non-experimental, one-group ex-post facto research design. Although one-group designs generate important information, they also leave unanswered questions about how much of the intervention is responsible for change. In contrast to randomized sampling designs, every eligible person in the group receives the same condition (Burt, Harrell, Newmark, Aron, & Jacobs, 1997; Rossi, Freeman, & Lipsey,

1999; Weiss, 1998). In this study, the condition received by each person was referral by either a criminal or a civil court to a battering intervention program within the county. Comparisons among dose-responses, or the number of legal sanctions, are feasible, as are comparisons between men who completed a battering intervention program and men who did not participate in a battering intervention program. In effect, this research compares and contrasts different kinds and combinations of sanctions used by the county to deter domestic violence related offenses (Babcock, Green, & Robie, 2004; Jerrell & Ridgely, 1999; Weiss, 1998).

DATA SOURCES AND DESCRIPTIONS

This study uses data extracted from two county operated computerized databases. The first is the County Court (CC) database, a system that documents criminal and civil case status and dispositions for cases filed in the county District Attorney's Office. Data include demographic characteristics such as age, race/ethnicity, level of court referral to battering intervention, prior court involvement in the county, and post court involvement in the county, including any cases of domestic violence filed within the county. The Family Violence Division (FVD) within the county District Attorney's Office developed the second database, FVD-DB. The division used the FVD-DB to track compliance of domestic violence offenders who are court ordered to battering intervention programs. The FVD-DB data included demographic information and the number of battering intervention program hours attended.

SAMPLE

The sampling frame for this study consisted of all male domestic violence offenders in the county who were court ordered to battering intervention program through either the criminal or the civil court (protective order) in 2001 ($n = 1802$). Only cases that involved male offenders with female victims identified as intimate partners (spouse, ex-spouse, girlfriend, or ex-girlfriend), were included in the sampling frame.

Women were not included in the sample. Unlike men, women arrested and court mandated to battering intervention programs tend to experience significant victimization from their male partners.

Additionally, the context of the violence appears to be very different for women arrested for domestic violence. For example, arrested women are more likely to report they were motivated to use violence as self-defense, to retaliate for past abuse, or to escape violence (Bair-Merritt, Crowne, Thompson, et al., 2010; Barnett, Lee, & Thelen, 1997; Dasgupta, 1999, 2002; Hamberger, 1997; Hamberger & Guse, 2002; Hamberger, Lohr, Bonge, & Tolin, 1997; Henning & Feder, 2004; Seamans, Rubin, & Stabb, 2007). The county courts processed cases for 29 women arrested for domestic violence in 2001. Consistent with the findings of Muftić and Bouffard (2007), the county courts were more likely to refer the women to anger management than battering intervention.

This study uses a probability sample drawn from the population of men in the county who were court ordered to attend battering intervention in 2001. To ensure equal representation of men who were involved with the civil and criminal courts for domestic violence offences, the study uses a probability sample selected through proportionate stratified random sampling. The stratification variable is the level of court involvement: criminal court or civil court. The probability sample consists of 607 men, approximately one third (34%) of the conceptual population. The first group consisted of men whose domestic violence cases were disposed of through the criminal courts between January 1, 2001 and December 31, 2001. Sentencing included a mandate to complete a battering intervention program. The second group was comprised of men who were respondents in protective order cases granted in civil court between January 1, 2001 and December 31, 2001, and who were court mandated to complete a battering intervention program (see Table 1).

Table 1. Stratification of Sample by Court Involvement in 2001

Court	Sampling Frame	Probability Sample
Civil	900	301
Criminal	902	306
Total	1802	607

DEPENDENT VARIABLE

The dependent variable is recidivism of domestic violence. The operational definition of recidivism is civil court involvement for protective orders, or criminal court involvement for domestic violence related offenses between the date of index case and December 31, 2006. The study uses two levels of measurement for the dependent variable: dichotomous and interval/ratio. As a dichotomous variable, recidivism is dummy coded as "1" = yes, and "0" = no. As an interval/ratio variable, the operational definition of recidivism is the number of years between the date of the offense of the index case and December 31, 2006. Cox proportional hazards regression modeling is used to examine recidivism as an interval ratio variable and will be discussed in detail later in this chapter. This study refers to men in the sample who were involved with the courts for domestic violence related offense or protective orders after the index case as "recidivists," and men in the sample who were not involved with the courts for domestic violence related offenses or protective orders after the index case as "non-recidivists."

Recidivism data were collected through the CC database used by the county to track court cases and dispositions. The database records were examined to determine if: 1) the county District Attorney filed new charges after the index case; or 2) any new protective order were filed with the civil court after the index case. Each man's name, date of birth, and case number was verified through case records in the CC database. In addition, access to non-public county information allowed for identification of domestic violence related crimes such as burglary, terroristic threats, sexual assault, kidnapping, stalking, and murder. When new cases filed after the index were identified, the offense date, charge, and case disposition were noted. This approach is consistent with prior research conducted on men who batter and recidivism of domestic violence (Bouffard & Muftić, 2007; Davis, Taylor, & Maxwell, 2000; Gondolf, 2002; Tollefson & Gross, 2006; Ventura & Davis, 2005; Wilson & Klein, 2006).

INDEPENDENT VARIABLES

Independent variables include demographic variables as well as variables related to court involvement and additional sanctions. Demographic variables in this study are limited to the only demographic information available on each case: age and race/ethnicity of the perpetrator. To examine the impact of legal sanctions on recidivism of domestic violence, this research uses the following independent variables: prior court involvement, index case court involvement (criminal or civil), incarceration for the index case, probation, hours attended in a battering intervention program, completion of a battering intervention program, court involvement after the index case, and incarceration after the index case. The Legal Sanctions Dose-Response Index score is the final measure, determining the cumulative level of dosage, or sanctions, imposed upon each individual in the study. A description of each variable follows.

Demographic Variables

Demographic variables include age and race/ethnicity. Age is an interval ratio variable, and is calculated as the age of the batterer at the time of the index offense. In descriptive analyses, age is also treated categorically and dummy coded into the following variables: Less than 21 years is coded as "1" = Yes and "0" = No; 21-30 years is coded as "1" = Yes and "0" = No; 31-40 years is coded as "1" = Yes and "0" = No; 41-50 years coded as "1" = Yes and "0" = No; and Greater than 50 years is coded as "1" = Yes and "0" = No.

Race/ethnicity is a nominal variable and notation is consistent with the Race/ethnicity designation in the CC and the FVD databases. Protective order applicants report race/ethnicity for respondents in protective order cases. In criminal cases, defendants identify their race/ethnicity through documentation presented to the court (e.g. driver's license), which is then noted in the CC database. For the purposes of this research, race/ethnicity was confirmed through the FVD-DB, which used Race/ethnicity as defined by the individual. Race/ethnicity is dummy coded as follows: White is coded "1" for White and "0" for Other Race. Black is coded "1" = Black and "0" = Other Race/ethnicity. Hispanic is a dummy variable with "1" = Hispanic and "0" = Other Race/ethnicity. The racial categories Asian and Other were initially dummy coded in the same manner. During preliminary analysis, however, the category Asian contained one individual and the category Other contained two individuals. Further investigation revealed that in one case, the individual self-identified as

Asian to the battering intervention program, but the CC database listed him as White. In two cases, the individuals self-identified as Other to the battering intervention program, but the CC database identified them as White. This study treats these three cases as exceptions to the self-identified classification of race/ethnicity; the legal system identification as White for race/ethnicity, rather than self-identified race or ethnicity, is included in the analysis. Additionally, because Black is the largest group in the sample, the analysis uses Black as the comparison group for the covariate race/ethnicity in the multivariate survival model.

Prior Court Involvement

Prior court involvement variables are nominal and include civil court (protective order) cases, and criminal court cases. For the purposes of this research, the variables are limited to court involvement, not the number of cases disposed of by the courts for each individual. Each variable is dummy coded as "1" = Yes and "0" = No.

Prior civil court involvement (protective order)

Prior civil court involvement consists of protective orders granted prior to the index case. This research does not take into consideration prior civil court involvement for non-domestic violence related cases such as property disputes or child custody. Prior court involvement for protective orders granted is dummy coded as "1" = Yes and "0" = No.

Prior criminal court involvement for domestic violence related offenses

Prior criminal court involvement for domestic violence related offenses are offenses in which the identified victim is or has been an intimate partner. Based upon the criminal case categories of the Texas Penal Code, domestic violence related offenses include violation of protective order, assault, sexual assault, kidnapping, stalking, terroristic threats, retaliation, burglary of a habitation, murder, and other offenses. Prior court involvement for domestic violence related offenses is treated as a dichotomous variable and coded as "1" = Yes and "0" = No.

Prior criminal court involvement for non-domestic violence related offenses

Prior criminal court involvement also includes non-domestic violence related offenses, which include such offenses as driving while intoxicated, theft, assault, sexual assault, kidnapping, stalking, murder, and other offenses for which the identified victim is not a known intimate partner. Prior criminal court involvement for non-domestic violence offenses is treated as dichotomous and dummy coded as "1" = Yes and "0" = No.

To explore the court involvement of the men in the sample, this study categorizes offenses filed with the county District Attorney's Office into felony level and misdemeanor level offenses. Modifications to the offense categories in the Texas Penal Code (Texas Penal Code, Title 5-9) incorporate domestic violence offense related cases into the broader categories. Table 2 details each felony offense variable, the type of felony criminal offenses committed by men in the sample, and the measure for each variable.

Table 2. Felony Criminal Offense Categories

Offense Variable	Criminal Offenses	Measure
Offenses against Persons	Murder; attempted murder; kidnapping; aggravated kidnapping; false imprisonment; unlawful restraint; indecency with a child; assault; aggravated assault; sexual assault; aggravated sexual assault; injury to a child; elderly or disabled individual; child endangerment; deadly conduct; terroristic threat; and violation of a protective order.	1 = Yes 0 = No
Offenses against Property	Arson; robbery; aggravated robbery; burglary of a habitation, business, or vehicle; criminal trespass; criminal mischief; theft; fraud; forgery; and credit card abuse.	1 = Yes 0 = No
Deadly Weapon Involved Offenses	Aggravated assault with a deadly weapon; aggravated sexual assault with a deadly weapon; and aggravated robbery with a deadly weapon.	1 = Yes 0 = No
Offenses against Public Administration	Bribery; retaliation; resisting arrest; evading arrest; escape; failure to register as a sex offender; tampering with evidence; and unauthorized absence from community corrections.	1 = Yes 0 = No

Table 2. Felony Criminal Offense Categories (Continued)

Offense Variable	Criminal Offenses	Measure
Offenses against Public Order	Stalking and engaging in organized crime.	1 = Yes 0 = No
Unlawful Weapon Offenses	Unlawful carrying weapons; taking weapons to places where weapons are prohibited; and unlawful possession of a weapon.	1 = Yes 0 = No
Drug Related Offenses	Possession of a controlled substance; possession of a controlled substance with intent to deliver; delivery of a controlled substance.	1 = Yes 0 = No
Alcohol Related Offenses	Driving while intoxicated.	1 = Yes 0 = No

Table 3 describes each misdemeanor offense variable, the type of misdemeanor criminal offenses committed by men in the sample, and the measure for each variable. In contrast to felony offenses, misdemeanors do not involve offenses that include a deadly weapon, although unlawful carrying or possession of a weapon is included. Misdemeanor drug related offenses are associated with personal drug use, and do not include intent to deliver or delivery of a controlled substance.

Table 3. Misdemeanor Criminal Offense Categories

Offense Variable	Criminal Offenses	Measure
Offenses against Persons	Unlawful restraint; indecent exposure; assault; injury to a child, deadly conduct; terroristic threat; and violation of a protective order.	1 = Yes 0 = No
Offenses against Property	Burglary of a vehicle or coin operated machine; criminal trespass; criminal mischief; theft; attempted theft; and fraud.	1 = Yes 0 = No
Offenses against Public Administration	Resisting arrest; evading arrest; escape; failure to identify; fictitious identification; and false statements.	1 = Yes 0 = No

Table 3. Misdemeanor Criminal Offense Categories (Continued)

Offense Variable	Criminal Offenses	Measure
Offenses against Public Order	Stalking, disorderly conduct; interference with an emergency phone call; harassment; telephone harassment; and prostitution.	1 = Yes 0 = No
Unlawful Weapon Offenses	Unlawful carrying of a weapon and unlawful possession of a weapon.	1 = Yes 0 = No
Drug Related Offenses	Possession of a controlled substance; obtaining a controlled substance; and inhalation of a chemical.	1 = Yes 0 = No
Alcohol Related Offenses	Driving while intoxicated.	1 = Yes 0 = No

Index Case: Legal Sanctions

This study defines the index case as the domestic violence case for which civil or criminal court ordered sanctions included referral to a battering intervention program. Legal sanctions invoked by the county for domestic violence related offenses include civil protective orders, arrest, incarceration, probation, and revocation of probation.

Index case court involvement

The stratification variable, index case court involvement, refers to the level of court that addressed the index case: civil court for protective orders and criminal court. Protective order index cases are cases in which victims petition the court for protection, or the cases are emergency protective orders served to incarcerated offenders. The variable is dichotomous and coded as "1" = Yes and "0" = No.

Criminal index cases are either Class A misdemeanor or felony offenses committed against a female intimate partner. The Texas Penal Code defines Class A misdemeanor assault as intentionally or knowingly: causing bodily injury to another; threatening another with imminent bodily injury; or causing physical contact with another when the person knows or should reasonably believe that the other will regard the contact as offensive or provocative (Texas Penal Code, Title

5, Chapter 22.01(a)(1-3)). In domestic violence cases, the assault becomes a felony if the person was previously convicted of domestic violence, caused serious bodily injury, or used or exhibited a deadly weapon during the commission of the assault (Texas Penal Code, Chapter 22.01 (b)(2) and Chapter 22.01(b)(1-2)). Because there are only five cases in which the index case is a felony offense, the analysis combines misdemeanor and felony offenses together as one variable, criminal court involvement.

Arrest
The variable Arrest for the index case is determined through documentation in the CC database, which indicates that an arrest occurred for the case of interest. For the purposes of this study, the index case is the case of interest. However, not all men in the sample experienced arrest for the index case. For example, those men who were court ordered to battering intervention through civil protective orders did not experience arrest because their index case was civil, not criminal. The variable Arrest is dichotomous and coded as "1" = Yes and "0" = No.

Incarceration for index case
The variable Incarceration for the index case is dichotomous and coded as "1" = Yes and "0" = No. Incarceration for the index case includes jail immediately after the arrest for domestic violence and jail for revocation of the terms of probation for the index case. For those men who spent time in jail for the index case, the length of their incarceration ranges from 1 day to 452 days. In descriptive analyses, incarceration is also dummy coded into categorical variables: 1-99 days is coded as "1" = Yes and "0" = No; 100-199 days is coded as "1" = Yes and "0" = No; 200-299 days is coded as "1" = Yes and "0" = No; and No incarceration is coded as "1" = Yes and "0" = No.

Probation for index case
The variable Probation for the index case is interval ratio and measured in months. Terms of probation range from 6 months to 24 months for misdemeanor domestic violence related cases and from 24 months to 120 months for felony domestic violence cases. In descriptive analyses, probation is also treated as a categorical variable and dummy coded as follows: Less than 12 months is coded as "1" = Yes and "0" = No;

13-23 months is coded as "1" = Yes and "0" = No; 24 months is coded as "1" = Yes and "0" = No; Greater than 24 months is coded as "1" = Yes and "0" = No; and No probation is coded as "1" = Yes and "0" = No. Compliance with the terms of probation entails following court orders for treatment, such as battering intervention, substance abuse or alcohol treatment, community service, court fines, orders to stay away from the victim, and any other conditions required as part of sentencing.

Revocation for index case

Revocation of probation can only occur if sentencing by the court includes probation. The variable Revocation for the index Case is categorical and coded as follows: Revocation is coded as "1" = Yes and "0" = No; No revocation is coded as "1" = Yes and "0" = No; and No probation is coded as "1" = Yes and "0" = No.

Battering Intervention Program Participation

The battering intervention program hours variable is an interval ratio variable. During the timeframe of the study, programs that received referrals from the courts in the county self-certify that they met minimum standards of the Battering Intervention and Prevention Project Guidelines (Texas Department of Criminal Justice, 1999). To meet minimum standards, approved programs used a psycho-educational group format. Group sessions addressed the societal and cultural structures that support violence and alternatives to violence. Individuals participating in approved battering intervention programs were required to attend a minimum of thirty-six hours of group intervention to complete a program (Texas Department of Criminal Justice, 1999). For men who participated to any extent in a battering intervention program, the hours attended ranged from 1.5 hours to 44 hours. To allow for comparisons between battering intervention program attendees and non-attendees and battering intervention program completers and non-completers, variables related to battering intervention are dummy coded as described in Table 4.

Table 4. Battering Intervention Program Participation

Variable	Battering Intervention Program Participation	Measure
No Show	Did not participate in court-ordered battering intervention.	1 = Yes 0 = No
Terminated	Completed intake but the program terminated the participant for non-compliance with program requirements.	1 = Yes 0 = No
Completed	Attended all required groups and completed the battering intervention program.	1 = Yes 0 = No

Legal Sanctions Dose-Response Index

The design of the Legal Sanctions Dose-Response Index captures "doses" of legal sanctions applied in response to the index case. The dose-response index includes the following variables: protective order, arrest, probation, revocation for violation of the terms of probation for the index case, and incarceration for either the index case or revocation of the terms of probation for the index case. The index treats each sanction as a dichotomous variable and assigns each sanction a value of one ("1" = Yes and "0" = No). There is a cumulative effect because some sanctions cannot take place without a prerequisite sanction. For example, a person cannot be on probation unless he is also arrested (two "doses"). Arrest and probation are prerequisites for revocation (three "doses"). In another scenario, someone could be arrested, incarcerated, have a protective order, and never be placed on probation because they served jail time (also three "doses"). Table 5 describes each variable within the index. Each intervention is dummy coded as "1" if the man experienced the specific intervention and "0" if the man did not experience the intervention. The sum of values is the number of sanctions received for the index case, or the cumulative dose-response on the Index. Because the group receiving one sanction is the largest group in the sample, this study uses the one-sanction group as the comparison group for the covariate categories of the Legal Sanctions Dose-Response Index in the multivariate survival model.

Table 5. Legal Sanctions Dose-Response Index

Variable	Description	Measure
Protective order	Sanctions for index case included civil court order with a finding of family violence.	1 = Yes 0 = No
Arrest	Sanctions for index case included arrest.	1 = Yes 0 = No
Probation	Sanctions for index case included probation.	1 = Yes 0 = No
Revocation	Sanctions for index case probation included revocation because of non-compliance with terms of probation.	1 = Yes 0 = No
Incarceration	Sanctions for index case include incarceration for a) index case, or b) revocation of terms of probation for index case.	1 = Yes 0 = No
Maximum possible score on index		5

Post-Index Case Court Involvement

Post-index case court involvement variables are nominal, and include domestic and non-domestic violence related criminal court cases. As with prior court involvement variables, these variables are limited to court involvement, not the number of cases disposed of by the courts for each individual. Each variable is dummy coded as "1" = Yes and "0" = No.

Post-index case criminal court involvement for domestic violence related offenses

Court involvement for domestic violence related offenses committed after the index case is inherent in the definition of recidivism. Domestic violence related criminal cases are cases in which the identified victim is or has been an intimate partner. Based upon the criminal case categories of the Texas Penal Code, domestic violence related cases include violation of protective order, assault, sexual assault, kidnapping, stalking, terroristic threats, retaliation, burglary of a habitation, murder, and other offenses. Post-index court involvement for domestic violence related offenses is dichotomous and coded as "1" = Yes and "0" = No.

Post-index case court involvement for non-domestic violence related offenses

Post-index case court involvement also includes non-domestic violence related offenses, which consist of driving while intoxicated, theft, assault, sexual assault, kidnapping, stalking, murder, and other offenses for which the identified victim is not a known intimate partner. Post-index court involvement for non-domestic violence related offenses is dummy coded as "1" = Yes and "0" = No.

To examine the post-index case court involvement of the men in the sample, this study categorizes offenses filed with the county District Attorney's Office into felony level and misdemeanor level offenses. As noted previously, Table 2 and Table 3 detail each felony and misdemeanor offense variable, criminal offenses committed by men in the sample, and the measure for each variable.

Incarceration During Follow-up Period

Incarceration is time spent incarcerated in jail or prison during the follow-up period. There are a number of reasons why a person may not have an opportunity to recidivate, including death, relocation, or incarceration. Because incarceration for any offense influences the opportunity for recidivism of domestic violence, and this information is the most readily available for the men in the sample, this research considers the amount of time spent incarcerated for any criminal offenses committed after the index case. For the 607 men in the sample, the length of time for incarceration during the follow-up period ranged from 1 day in jail to, in the case of at least one man, incarceration in prison during almost the entire follow-up period. For the chi-square analysis, incarceration is dummy coded as "1" = Yes and "0" = No. The Cox proportional hazards regression model treats incarceration an interval/ratio variable measured in terms of years in jail or prison during the follow-up period of the study.

METHODS

Frequency distributions are constructed from the data to describe characteristics of the population of men in the sample, including age, race/ethnicity, prior court involvement, index case court involvement, incarceration for the index case, probation, revocation of probation, battering intervention program participation, and incarceration in jail or prison for offenses other than the index case during the follow-up period. Additionally, frequency distributions illustrate the type of felony and misdemeanor offenses committed by men in the sample both before and after the index case. The nature, association, and strength of relationships between the dependent variable, recidivism of domestic violence, and the independent variables are determined through chi-square tests and the *phi* coefficient. Chi-square addresses the issue of whether or not there is a relationship between the variables; the *phi* coefficient estimates the effect size or strength of statistically significant relationships (Grissom & Kim, 2005). To examine the differences between recidivists and non-recidivists, the study employs a chi-square analysis for dichotomous variables, and the *phi* coefficient to determine effect size of statistically significant relationships.

The study also employs *t*-tests to examine differences in the means for interval/ratio or continuous variables and Hedge's *g* to determine effect sizes. However, it is important to caution that significant differences may not be due only to recidivism because men in the sample are not randomly assigned to recidivist and non-recidivist group membership. Other unmeasured variables may possibly either hide or add to any statistical significance results (Garson, 2008b).

As noted earlier, this study employs the Cox proportional hazards model, using recidivism as the status variable and the length of time a man maintained his non-recidivism status as the time variable. The Cox proportional hazards regression model is a semi-parametric approach because the model assumes no particular type of distribution for the survival times. However, there is a strong assumption that the effects of the different variables on survival are constant (proportional) over time (Allison, 1999; Altman, 1991; Garson, 2008a).

The Cox proportional hazards regression model allows for data analysis where the outcome variable is time until an event occurs, in this case, recidivism (Clark, Bradburn, Love, & Altman, 2003). One benefit of the model is that it provides a way to deal with men in the sample who are considered non-recidivists because they were not been involved in the courts for domestic violence related offenses by the end of the follow-up period, December 31, 2006. Men in the sample with this unknown event time are *right censored* cases. They are not involved with the courts for domestic violence related offenses during the time-period under study and their recidivism, if it occurs, is after the follow-up period (Altman, 1991; Clark et al., 2003; Keiley & Martin, 2005). In these cases, censoring is non-informative. That is, those censored because they were not involved with the courts for domestic violence offenses during the follow-up period may be just as likely to reoffend as those who remain in the study (Clark, et. al, 2003). In their study on predicting recidivism,

The Cox proportional hazards regression model describes the relationship between the target event incidence, expressed by the hazard function, and a set of covariates (Bradburn, Clark, Love, & Altman, 2003). The hazard function, or hazard ratio, is the conditional probability that an individual under observation will experience the target event, in this case recidivism, during the designated time, given that they have not experienced it up to that point in time (Allison, 1999; Altman, 1991; Bradburn et al., 2003; Keiley & Martin, 2005).

LIMITATIONS OF THE STUDY

While this study contributes an important examination of the impact of legal sanctions on recidivism of male perpetrators of domestic violence, there are some limitations. The design is a non-experimental one-group ex post facto design and, whereas comparisons are made within the study group (such as comparisons between recidivists and non-recidivists or battering intervention program completers and non-completers), it is impossible to control for all possible differences.

Another limitation is the use of only one source to determine recidivism status: official records for civil and criminal court cases filed with the county District Attorney's office. Basing outcome measures such as recidivism solely on official records is problematic and likely underestimates recidivism. Because victims may not reach out to authorities when domestic violence occurs, or police may not detect or arrest in incidents of domestic violence, it is possible that men in the sample may not have come to the attention of either the civil or criminal courts for new acts of violence (Bouffard & Muftić, 2007;

Buzawa & Buzawa, 2003; Davis, Smith, & Nickles, 1998; Johnson, 2008). Moreover, if a man changed residence and moved outside the county, the move would not necessarily be in the official record. Consequently, the county would have no record of any subsequent domestic violence related offenses occurring outside the county. Court records for the follow-up period also indicated that some of the men in the sample were deceased. For example, according to court records in one case, the spouse of one of the men in the sample shot and killed him after he assaulted her. It is possible, however, that county records did not capture all deaths among the men in the sample.

The absence of information related to individual characteristics of the men in the sample and characteristics of the county's response to domestic violence is also a limitation of this study. As noted earlier, the data do not include individual characteristics such as alcohol or substance abuse, employment stability, psychological disorders, or measures of stake in conformity. Individual characteristics could provide additional information on risk factors for recidivism. Additionally, stake in conformity measures such as education, residency, employment, home ownership, and marital status could provide insight into social bonding and other factors that may influence recidivism (Feder & Dugan, 2002; Sherman et al., 1992). Because the primary data sources for this research are limited to the county databases, information about county policies and practices to coordinate services to victims and hold batterers accountable are beyond the scope of this study. Additionally, because of the variation among communities in their response to domestic violence (Gondolf, 2002), as well as the limitations of this research, the results are specific to the county and may not generalize to other communities. Finally, by design, the Cox proportional hazard regression model assumes that all are at risk for recidivism. The censored cases of men who have not recidivated are not informative, because it is unknown whether the men will recidivate in the future.

SUMMARY

The analyses for this research is designed to examine the impact of legal sanctions upon the relative risk recidivism of men who committed domestic violence related offenses in a Texas county, using a non-experimental, one-group ex-post facto research design. This study uses data extracted from two computerized databases made available through the county District Attorney's Office. The sampling frame consisted of all male domestic violence offenders in the county who were court ordered to attend battering intervention programs. The sample selection was through proportionate randomized sampling using the level of court involvement as the stratification variable. The dependent variable is recidivism of civil and criminal domestic violence related offenses during the five-year follow-up period. Independent variables include the following: age; race/ethnicity; prior court involvement for domestic violence related offenses (civil court and criminal court); prior court involvement for non-domestic violence offenses; legal sanctions for the index case such as arrest, protective orders, incarceration, probation, and revocation; participation in a battering intervention program; number of sanctions imposed for the index case, as measured by the Legal Sanctions Dose-Response Index; post-index case criminal court involvement for non-domestic violence related offenses; and incarceration for any offense committed during the follow-up period. This chapter also lists the hypotheses proposed for the study and discusses the analyses, which include frequency distributions, chi-square bivariate analyses, *t*-test for independent samples, and Cox PH regression models.

CHAPTER FIVE

Characteristics and Court Involvement of Men in the Study

This chapter discusses the characteristics of the 607 men included in the study, any civil or criminal court involvement prior to the index case, and the legal sanctions imposed through the disposition of the index case. Frequency distributions include the variables age, race, prior court involvement, court involvement for the index case, incarceration for the index case, probation, battering intervention program attendance, post court involvement, and incarceration in jail or prison during follow-up period.

Demographic Characteristics

Table 6 presents the frequency distributions of the demographic characteristics of the 607 men in the sample. The mean age was 33.9 (SD = 9.6). Of the 607 men in the sample, 232 (38.2%) were between the ages of 21 and 30 years old, followed by 200 men between the ages of 31 and 40 years old (32.9 %). The remaining men were either younger than 21 years old or older than 40 years old.

The races of the men in the sample present an interesting contrast to the general population of the county. At the time of the 2000 Census, county residents were predominately white (56.4%). Black residents made up the next largest group (25.5%), followed by Hispanic residents (18.1%) (U. S. Census Bureau, 2000). In the sample of 607 men, however, the smallest group was comprised of white men (26.3%). The

largest group was comprised of Black men (40.2 %), followed by
Hispanic men (33.5%).

**Table 6. Demographic Characteristics of Male Perpetrators of
Domestic Violence, 2001 (N = 607)**

Variable	*n*	Percent[a]
Age		
Mean Age in years	33.9	
(SD)	(9.6)	
Race		
Black	244	40.2
Hispanic	204	33.6
White	159	26.2

[a] *Note*: Percentages may not sum to 100% due to rounding.

Prior Court Involvement

Prior court involvement includes domestic violence related cases such as
protective orders in the civil court, as well as domestic violence related
cases and non-domestic violence related cases in the criminal courts (see
Table 7). The majority of the sample (63.1%) had some court
involvement prior to the index case. Sixty-three men (10.4%) had prior
civil court involvement for protective orders and 64 (10.5%) were
involved in the courts for criminal domestic violence related offenses.
More than half (59.0%) of the men in the sample were involved in the
courts for non-domestic violence related offenses prior to the index case.

Criminal Court Involvement Prior to Index Case

More than half the sample, 388 of 607 men (63.9%), had some criminal
court involvement prior to the index case. According to county records,
217 (35.7%) had prior court involvement at the felony level for non-
domestic violence related offenses and 301 (49.6%) had prior court
involvement at the misdemeanor level. As shown in Table 8, 64
(10.5%) of the 607 men in the sample had prior criminal court
involvement for domestic violence related cases. While few men had
domestic violence related criminal court involvement prior to the index
case, 358 men in the sample (59.0%) had prior court involvement for
non-domestic violence related offenses. Almost half of the men in the

sample (49.6%) were involved with the courts for non-domestic violence related misdemeanor offenses, prior to the index case.

Table 7. Prior Court Involvement of Male Perpetrators of Domestic Violence, 2001 (N = 607)

Variable	*n*	Percent[a]
Any Court Involvement Prior to Index Case (including Civil Court)		
Involvement	388	63.1
No involvement	219	36.1
Types of Court Involvement Prior to Index Case[b]		
Domestic Violence Related		
Civil (Protective Order)		
Involvement	63	10.4
No involvement	544	89.6
Domestic Violence Related Criminal		
Involvement	64	10.5
No involvement	543	89.5
Non-Domestic Violence Related Criminal		
Involvement	358	59.0
No involvement	249	41.0

[a] *Note*: Percentages may not sum to 100% due to rounding.
[b] Categories are not mutually exclusive; persons may be counted in more than one category.

Table 8. Prior Criminal Court Involvement of Male Perpetrators of Domestic Violence, 2001 (N = 607)

Variable	Felony Offenses[a]		Misdemeanor Offenses[a]		Total Involvement[a]	
	n	%	*n*	%	*n*	%
Men involved in the courts for domestic violence related offenses	30	4.9	38	6.3	64	10.5

Table 8. Prior Criminal Court Involvement of Male Perpetrators of Domestic Violence, 2001 (N = 607) (Continued)

Variable	Felony Offenses[a]		Misdemeanor Offenses[a]		Total Involvement[a]	
	n	%	*n*	%	*n*	%
Men involved in the courts for non-domestic violence related offenses	217	35.7	301	49.6	358	59.0
Total men involved in the courts for any prior offense	229	37.7	313	51.6	388	63.9

[a] Note: Totals will not sum to 100% because categories are not mutually exclusive; persons may be counted in more than one category.

Table 9 presents frequencies and percentages of the types of cases represented in prior criminal court involvements. Out of the 607 men in the sample, 125 men (20.4%) were involved with the courts for misdemeanor level offenses against persons prior to the index case.

Table 9. Male Perpetrators of Domestic Violence Criminal Court Involvement Prior to Index Case, 2001 (N = 607)

Variable	Felony Offenses[a]		Misdemeanor Offenses[a]	
	n	%	*n*	%
Men involved with the courts for domestic violence related offenses:				
Against persons	17	2.8	27	4.4
Against property	3	.5	10	1.6
Deadly weapon involved (offenses against persons or property)	11	1.8		
Against public administration			3	.5
Against public order			2	.3

Table 9. Male Perpetrators of Domestic Violence Criminal Court Involvement Prior to Index Case, 2001 (N = 607) (Continued)

Variable	Felony Offenses[a]		Misdemeanor Offenses[a]	
	n	%	*n*	%
Men involved with the courts for non-domestic violence offenses:				
Against persons	58	9.6	124	20.4
Against property	103	17.0	103	17.0
Deadly weapon involved (offenses against persons or property)	56	9.2		
Against public administration	23	3.8	66	10.9
Against public order			17	2.8
Unlawful weapons	4	.7	36	5.9
Drugs	53	8.7	77	12.7
Alcohol	11	1.8	78	12.9

[a] *Note*: Totals will not sum to 100% because categories are not mutually exclusive; persons may be counted in more than one category. Of the sample of 607 men, none was involved with the courts for prior domestic violence related offenses related to unlawful weapons, drugs, or alcohol. The table does not include these categories.

The next largest groups consisted of 103 men (17.0%) whose court involvement was for felony offenses against property, and 103 men (17.0%) whose court involvement was for misdemeanor offenses against property. Prior to their index cases, men in the sample were more likely to use deadly weapons non-domestic violence offenses. Fifty-six men (9.2%) used deadly weapons in non-domestic violence related offenses compared to 11 (1.8%) men who were involved with the courts for use of deadly weapons in domestic violence related cases prior to their index case.

Legal Sanctions for the Index Case

The stratification variable, index case court involvement, refers to the level of court that addressed the index case: civil court for protective orders and criminal court. As noted previously, protective order cases are cases in which victims petition the court for protection, or the cases are emergency protective orders served to offenders while they are still in jail after an arrest for domestic violence. Table 10 displays frequencies for the legal sanctions received for the index case. Of the 607 men in the sample, 301 (49.6%) had the index case disposed of through a civil court in the form of a protective order. Criminal index cases are either Class A misdemeanor or felony offenses committed against a female intimate partner. Of the 607 men, 306 (50.4%) had the index case disposed of through the criminal court.

Over half of the 607 men (56%) were arrested for the index case. Not all arrested, however, spent time in jail. Incarceration in jail for the index case includes time spent immediately following arrest, time spent because of sentencing by the court for the index case, and time spent due to revocation of probation. Out of 607 men, 107 (17.6%) spent time in jail the index case. The number of days served following their arrest for the index case ranged from 1 day to 292 days. The mean number of days served in jail for the index case was 61.1 days   (SD = 56.5). Revocation of probation for the index case was the primary reason for lengthy periods served in jail.

Of the 607 men in the sample, the courts sentenced 307 to probation for the index case. Sentences ranged from 9 months to 10 years, depending upon the severity of the offense. The mean time on probation was 19.6 months (*SD* = 10.3). While approximately 116 men (19.0%) had their probation for the index case revoked, available court documentation did not specify if the revocation was due to recidivism of domestic violence. Revocation could also be a court response to additional arrests for non-domestic violence related offenses or noncompliance with court orders such as terms of probation.

Table 10. Legal Sanctions for Index Case of Male Perpetrators of Domestic Violence, 2001 (N = 607)

Variable	*n*	Percent[a]
Index Case Court Involvement		
Civil Court (Protective Order)	301	49.6
Criminal Court	306	50.4
Arrest for Index Case		
Arrest	340	44.0
No Arrest	267	56.0

Table 10. **Legal Sanctions for Index Case of Male Perpetrators of Domestic Violence, 2001 (N = 607) (Continued)**

Variable	n	Percent[a]
Incarcerated in Jail for Index Case		
Incarcerated	107	17.6
Not incarcerated	500	82.4
Mean days incarcerated in jail for index case	61.1	
(*SD*)	(56.5)	
Probation for Index Case		
Probation	307	50.6
No Probation	300	49.4
Revocation of Probation for Index Case		
Revocation	116	19.1
No revocation	191	31.5
Not on probation	300	49.4

[a] *Note*: Percentages may not sum to 100% due to rounding.
[b] Categories are not mutually exclusive; persons may be counted in more than one category.

Battering Intervention Program Participation

All 607 men in the sample were court ordered to participate in a battering intervention program. Despite the court order, however, more than half of the men (59.5%) had no contact with any of the battering intervention programs in the county. Seventy-six men (12.5%) began participation in a program but did not complete. (see Table 11).

Table 11. **Battering Intervention Program Participation of Male Perpetrators of Domestic Violence, 2001 (N = 607)**

Variable	n	Percent[a]
No contact with a battering intervention program	361	59.5
Did not complete a battering intervention program	76	12.5
Completed a battering intervention program	170	28.0
Mean battering intervention program participation hours	29.3	
(*SD*)	(12.5)	

[a] *Note*: Percentages may not sum to 100% due to rounding.

There are two possible explanations for non-completion. One explanation is that the men voluntarily dropped out of the program. Another is that the program terminated their participation for non-compliance with program requirements. The remaining 170 men (28.0%) completed the program. For those who participated for any length of time in a battering intervention program, the mean number of counseling hours for the 36-hour programs was 29.3 (SD = 12.5).

Post- Index Case Court Involvement

During the five-year follow-up period, 292 men (48.1%) of the 607 men in the sample had some court involvement after the index case. As shown in Table 12, fifty-nine men (9.7%) had protective orders granted against them through the civil courts. Additionally, 154 men (43.8%) were involved with the criminal courts for domestic violence related offenses. About one-third of the men (33.4%) were also involved with the criminal courts for non-domestic violence related offenses. Incarceration during the follow-up period affected 267 men (43%) with a mean of 1.3 (SD = 1.7) years spent in jail or prison.

Table 12. Post-Index Case Court Involvement of Male Perpetrators of Domestic Violence, 2001 (N = 607)

Variable	n	Percent[a]
Post-Index Case Court Involvement (Including Civil Court)		
Involvement	292	48.1
No involvement	315	51.9
Types of Post-Index Case Court Involvement[b]		
Domestic Violence Related		
Civil (Protective Order)		
Involvement	59	9.7
No involvement	548	90.3
Criminal		
Involvement	154	25.4
No involvement	453	74.6
Non-Domestic Violence Related		
Criminal		
Involvement	203	33.4
No involvement	404	66.6

Table 12. **Post-Index Case Court Involvement of Male Perpetrators of Domestic Violence, 2001 (N = 607) (Continued)**

Variable	n	Percent[a]
Post-Index Case Incarceration During Follow-up Period		
Incarcerated	267	44.0
Not incarcerated	340	56.0
Mean Years incarcerated during follow-up period	0.6	
(SD)	(1.3)	

[a] *Note*: Percentages may not sum to 100% due to rounding.
[b] Categories are not mutually exclusive; persons may be counted in more than one category.

Criminal Court Involvement Post- Index Case

Almost half of the 607 men in the sample were involved in the criminal court system during the five-year follow-up period. As shown in Table 13, 277 (45.6%) were involved in the criminal court system after the index case. Included in this number are the 154 men (25.4%) who committed domestic violence related offenses that were disposed of through the criminal courts. These men are included in the recidivating group discussed in the next section. Ninety men (14.8%) in the sample were involved with the criminal courts for felony level domestic violence related offenses and 89 men (14.7%) were involved in the courts for misdemeanor level offenses after the index case.

Table 13. **Post-Index Case Criminal Court Involvement of Male Perpetrators of Domestic Violence, 2001 (N = 607)**

Variable	Felony Offenses[a]		Misdemeanor Offenses[a]		Total Involvement[a]	
	n	%	n	%	n	%
Men involved in the courts for domestic violence related offenses	90	14.8	89	14.7	154	25.4
Men involved in the courts for non-domestic violence related offenses	137	22.6	131	21.6	203	33.4
Total men involved in the courts for any offenses after index case	196	32.3	188	31.0	277	45.6

[a] *Note:* Totals will not sum to 100% because categories are not mutually exclusive; persons may be counted in more than one category.

Table 14 presents frequencies and percentages of case types represented in criminal court involvements post-index case. Most non-domestic violence court involvement was for felony level offenses against property committed by 49 men (8.0%), followed by misdemeanor level offenses against public administration committed by 42 men (6.9%). Forty men (6.6%) were involved in the court system for felony level drug related offenses and 18 men (3.0%) were involved in the court system for misdemeanor level drug related offenses. Eleven men in the sample (1.8%) were involved in the court system for felony level alcohol related offenses and 25 men (4.1%) were involved in the courts at the misdemeanor level for alcohol related offenses.

Table 14. Male Perpetrators of Domestic Violence Post-Index Case Criminal Court Involvement, 2001 (N = 607)

Variable	Felony Offenses[a]		Misdemeanor Offenses[a]	
	n	%	*n*	%
Men involved with the courts for domestic violence related offenses:				
Against persons	83	13.7	89	14.7
Against property	2	.3	1	.2
Deadly weapon involved (offenses against persons or property)	9	1.5		
Against public order	1	.2		
Men involved with the courts for non-domestic violence related offenses:				
Against persons	26	4.3	18	3.0
Against property	48	7.9	42	6.9
Deadly weapon involved (offenses against persons or property)	26	4.3		
Against public administration	29	4.8	42	6.9
Against public order			9	1.5
Unlawful weapons	2	.3	8	1.3
Drugs	39	6.4	18	3.0
Alcohol	10	1.6	23	3.8

[a] *Note:* Totals will not sum to 100% because categories are not mutually exclusive; persons may be counted in more than one category. Of the sample of 607 men, none was involved with the courts for prior domestic violence related offenses against public administration or domestic violence related offenses such as unlawful weapons, drugs, or alcohol. The table does not include these categories.

CHAPTER SIX

Comparisons between Recidivists and Non-Recidivists

This chapter presents the statistical analyses comparing recidivists of domestic violence with non-recidivists using bivariate cross tabulations. To examine differences in the means for interval/ratio or continuous variables, this study employs *t*-tests. To measure effect sizes, this study uses Hedge's *g*. The chi-square tests of significance determine the probability of associations of nominal-level and dichotomous variables with recidivism of domestic violence. The *phi* coefficient reflects the strength of the associations. In addition to the descriptive statistics and analysis of mean differences, this study uses Cox proportional hazards regression analysis to predict the risk of recidivism of domestic violence over time, comparing the number of community legal sanctions (or dose-response) imposed for the index case.

During the follow-up period, 69.8% of the 607 men in the sample were not involved with either the civil or the criminal courts for domestic violence related offenses. The remaining 184 men in the sample (30.2%) were involved with the courts and met the study's criteria for recidivism of domestic violence: any cases filed in the county for domestic violence related criminal offenses, or any protective orders processed by the county District Attorney's office after the index case. The number of days from the index case to recidivism ranges from 1 day to 2805 days. The mean number of days to recidivism is 467.8 days and the median number of days is 223.0 days.

To examine differences between recidivists and non-recidivists, the study uses independent sample t-tests (and Hedge's g as the effect size) for interval-ratio or continuous variables, and chi-square analysis (and the *phi* coefficient as the effect size) for dichotomous variables. The study uses Cohen's (1992) operational definitions for effect sizes (the strength of the relationship between the dependent variable recidivism and the independent variable). For Hedge's g, the operational definition for a "small" effect size is about .20, a "moderate" effect size is about .50, and a "large" effect size is approximately .80. For the *phi* coefficient, the operational definition for a "small" effect size is about .10, a "moderate" effect size is about .30, and a "large" effect size is approximately .50.

INDEPENDENT SAMPLES T-TEST RESULTS

The t-test for independent samples compares the means for recidivists and non-recidivists on the continuous variables age, number of days served in jail for the index case, months served on probation, hours attended in a battering intervention program, and days incarcerated during the follow-up period (see Table 15). The results of comparisons of the means indicate time served in jail for the index case intervention ($t = .832$, $\rho > .05$, $g = .075$) and months served on probation are not significant ($t = -.673$, $\rho > .05$, $g = .057$). However, recidivists and non-recidivists differ significantly with a small effect size in the means for age and a moderate effect sizes for mean hours attended in a battering intervention program, and for mean number of days incarcerated during the follow-up period. Compared to non-recidivists, recidivists, on average, were younger ($t = -1.966$, $\rho \leq .05$, $g = .177$), with a small effect size for age. Compared to non-recidivists, recidivists participated in fewer hours of battering intervention ($t = -3.326$, $\rho \leq .01$, $g = -.295$), and spent more years incarcerated during the follow-up period ($t = 5.308$, $\rho \leq .01$, $g = .487$).

Table 15. Differences Between Recidivists and Non-Recidivists on Selected Variables: Independent Samples *t*-Test

Variable	Recidivists		Non-Recidivists		*t* (605)
	M	*SD*	*M*	*SD*	
Age (years)	32.7	9.4	34.4	9.7	-1.966*
Time served in jail for index case (days)	12.5	30.4	10.0	34.3	.832
Probation (months)	9.4	13.9	10.1	11.4	-.673
Battering Intervention Program attendance (hours)	8.5	14.6	13.3	16.9	-3.326**
Incarceration during follow-up period (years)	1.0	1.6	.4	1.1	5.308***

*$p \leq .05$. **$p \leq .01$. ***$p \leq .001$

CHI-SQUARE TEST RESULTS

Chi-square Test results for Race/Ethnicity and Recidivism

The chi-square test results reveal statistically significant differences between recidivists and non-recidivists on most of the dichotomous variables. However, many of the measure of association results are within the "small" range, which indicate that, despite statistical significance, the strength of the relationships are weak.

As shown in Table 16, the relationship between race/ethnicity and recidivism is significant for Black and Hispanic men in the sample, but not for White men ($\chi^2 = .412$, $df = 1$, $\rho > .05$; $\varphi = .026$). A significant relationship exists between being Black and recidivism ($\chi^2 = 6.392$, $df = 1$, $\rho \leq .05$; $\varphi = .103$). Black men are over-represented in the group of men who recidivated compared those who did not recidivate. Approximately 47.8% of recidivists were Black compared to 36.2% of non-recidivists, a difference of 11.6 percentage points. A significant relationship also exists between being Hispanic and recidivism indicating that Hispanic men were less likely to recidivate ($\chi^2 = 4.106$,

$df = 1$, $\rho \le .05$; $\varphi = .082$). About 27.7% of recidivists were Hispanic compared to 36.5% of non-recidivists, a difference of 8.8 percentage points. However, the measures of association for both Black men and Hispanic men indicate that the strength of the association between race and recidivism of domestic violence is weak.

Table 16. Differences Between Recidivists and Non-Recidivists on Race/Ethnicity: Bivariate Analysis (Chi-square Test)

Variable	Recidivists		Non-Recidivists		Total		χ^2
	n	%[a]	n	%[a]	n	%[a]	
Race/Ethnicity							
Black	88	47.8	156	36.2	244	40.2	6.392*
Hispanic	51	27.7	153	36.5	204	33.6	4.106*
White	45	24.5	114	27.0	159	26.2	.412
Total	184	100.0	423	99.7	607	100.0	

[a] *Note*: Percentages may not sum to 100% due to rounding.
*$p \le .05$ **$p \le .01$ ***$p \le .001$

Chi-square Tests for Prior Court Involvement and Recidivism

For the purposes of this study, prior court involvement included any involvement with the civil courts related to prior protective orders and any court involvement for prior criminal offenses, including felony or misdemeanor offenses. Men in the sample who were recidivists were more likely to have been involved with the courts prior to the index case than men who were not recidivists (see Table 17). Combining prior civil court involvement for protective orders and prior criminal court involvement for domestic violence related offenses, approximately 86.4% of the recidivists in this study had a history of domestic violence indicated in the county database. Additionally, a significant relationship exists between court involvement of any type and recidivism ($\chi^2 = 10.221$, $df = 1$, $\rho \le .001$; $\varphi = .130$). Approximately 73.4% of recidivists were involved in the courts prior to the index case compared to 59.8% of non-recidivists, a difference of 13.6 percentage points. The measure of association between prior court involvement and recidivism, however, indicates that the strength of the association is weak.

Table 17. Differences Between Recidivists and Non-Recidivists on Prior Court Involvement: Bivariate Analysis (Chi-square Test)

Variable	Recidivists		Non-Recidivists		Total		χ^2
	n	%[a]	*n*	%[a]	*n*	%[a]	
Any Prior Court Involvement							10.221***
Involvement	135	73.4	253	59.8	388	63.9	
No involvement	49	26.6	170	40.2	219	36.1	
Total	184	100.0	423	100.0	607	100.0	
Type of Prior Court Involvement[b]							
DV[c] Related							
Protective Order							9.967**
Involvement	30	16.3	33	7.8	63	10.4	
No involvement	154	83.7	390	92.2	544	89.6	
Total	184	100.0	423	100.0	607	100.0	
Criminal							9.290**
Involvement	30	16.3	34	8.0	64	10.5	
No involvement	154	83.7	389	92.0	543	89.5	
Total	184	100.0	423	100.0	607	100.0	
Non-DV Related							
Criminal							6.758*
Involvement	123	66.8	235	55.6	358	59.0	
No involvement	61	33.2	188	44.4	249	41.0	
Total	184	100.0	423	100.0	607	100.0	

[a] *Note*: Percentages may not sum to 100% due to rounding.

[b] Categories are not mutually exclusive; some men were involved with the courts for more than one type of case.

[c] DV = Domestic Violence

*$p \leq .05$ **$p \leq .01$ ***$p \leq .001$

Types of offenses represented in prior court involvement are also statistically significant. A significant relationship exists between prior court involvement for protective orders and recidivism ($\chi^2 = 9.967$, $df = 1$, $\rho \leq .01$; $\varphi = .128$), prior court involvement for domestic violence related cases and recidivism (χ^2 = 9.290, df = 1, $\rho \leq .01$; φ = .124), and prior court involvement for non-domestic violence related offenses and recidivism (χ^2 = 6.758, df = 1, $\rho \leq .05$; φ = .106). Although statistically significant, the measure of association for each of these variables with recidivism suggests that the strength of each of the relationships is weak.

Chi-Square Tests for Prior Criminal Court Involvement for Felony Offenses and Recidivism

As presented in Table 18, the relationship between prior court involvement for felony domestic violence related offenses is not significant (χ^2 = 1.402, df = 1, $\rho > .05$; φ = .048). However, a significant relationship does exist between prior court involvement for felony non-domestic violence related offenses and recidivism of domestic violence related offenses (χ^2 = 7.866, df = 1, $\rho \leq .01$; φ = .114). Approximately 44.0% of the recidivists were involved with the felony courts for non-domestic violence related offenses prior to the index case compared 32.2% of the non-recidivists, a percentage point difference of 11.8. Combining both domestic violence related and non-domestic violence related offenses, recidivists were more likely than non-recidivists were to be involved with the felony courts for any offenses prior to the index case.

Table 18. Differences Between Domestic Violence Recidivists and Non-Recidivists on Prior Criminal Court Involvement for Felony Offenses: Bivariate Analysis (Chi-square Test)

Variable	Recidivists		Non-Recidivists		Total		χ^2
	n	%	n	%	n	%	
Court involvement for DV [a] related offenses							1.402
Involvement	12	6.5	18	4.3	30	4.9	
No involvement	172	93.5	405	95.7	577	95.1	
Total	184	100.0	423	100.0	607	100.0	
Court involvement for non-DV related offenses							7.866**
Involvement	81	44.0	136	32.2	217	35.7	
No involvement	103	56.0	287	67.8	390	64.3	
Total	184	100.0	423	100.0	607	100.0	

Table 18. Differences Between Domestic Violence Recidivists and Non-Recidivists on Prior Criminal Court Involvement for Felony Offenses: Bivariate Analysis (Chi-square Test) (Continued)

Variable	Recidivists		Non-Recidivists		Total		χ^2
	n	%	*n*	%	*n*	%	
Prior court involvement							6.125*
for any felony offenses							
Involvement	83	45.1	146	34.5	229	37.7	
No involvement	101	54.9	277	65.5	378	62.3	
Total	184	100.0	423	100.0	607	100.0	

Note: Categories are not mutually exclusive; some men were involved with the courts for more than one type of criminal case.

[a]DV = Domestic Violence

*$p \leq .05$. **$p \leq .01$.

Despite the statistically significant relationship between criminal court involvement for felony offenses prior to the index case, the strength of the association is weak ($\chi^2 = 6.125$, $df = 1$, $p \leq .05$; $\varphi = .100$). About 45.1% of the recidivists were involved with the courts for felony offenses prior to the index case compared to 34.5% of the non-recidivists, a difference of 9.6 percentage points.

As shown in Table 19, there are no significant differences between recidivists and non-recidivists on prior court involvement for domestic violence related felony offenses such as offenses against persons ($\chi^2 = 2.322$, $df = 1$, $p > .05$; $\varphi = .062$) and use of a deadly weapon ($\chi^2 = .780$, $df = 1$, $p > .05$; $\varphi = .036$). Additionally, no significant differences exist between recidivists and non-recidivists on prior court involvement for non-domestic violence related felony offenses such as: offenses against persons ($\chi^2 = 1.055$, $df = 1$, $p > .05$; $\varphi = .042$); use of a deadly weapon ($\chi^2 = 1.508$, $df = 1$, $p > .05$; $\varphi = .050$); possession of unlawful weapons ($\chi^2 = .739$, $df = 1$, $p > .05$; $\varphi = .035$); drug related offenses ($\chi^2 = .418$, $df = 1$, $p > .05$; $\varphi = .026$); and alcohol related offenses ($\chi^2 = .049$, $df = 1$, $p > .05$; $\varphi = .009$). However, significant differences exist between recidivists and non-recidivists on prior criminal court involvement for felony offenses against property for both domestic violence and non-domestic violence related offenses and for offenses against public administration.

While prior domestic violence related offenses against property are statistically significant, only 1.5% of recidivists (compared to 0% of non-recidivists) were involved with the courts for these offenses. Compared with non-recidivists, recidivists are more likely to be involved with the criminal courts for prior non-domestic violence related offenses against property ($\chi2$ = 6.430, df = 1, $\rho \leq .05$; ϕ = .103). Approximately 22.8% of recidivists were involved with the criminal courts for felony non-domestic violence related offenses against property compared to 14.4% of non-recidivists, a difference of 8.4 percentage points. As with other variables, the measure of association indicates that the relationship is weak. Finally, recidivists were more likely than non-recidivists to have prior involvement with the courts for non-domestic violence related felony offenses against public administration ($\chi2$ = 7.773, df = 1, $\rho \leq .01$; ϕ = .113). The percentages for court involvement for these offenses are low with 7.1% of recidivists and 2.4% of non-recidivists involved with the criminal court for non-domestic violence related offenses associated with offenses against public administration, a difference of 4.7 percentage points. The measure of association between recidivism of domestic violence and prior involvement with the courts for felony against public administration is also weak.

Chi-Square Tests for Criminal Court Involvement Misdemeanor Offenses Prior to Index Case and Recidivism

Unlike court involvement for felony offenses, a significant relationship exists between court involvement for misdemeanor domestic violence related offenses and recidivism of domestic violence. However, the relationship between prior court involvement for misdemeanor non-domestic violence related offenses is not significant (χ^2 = 2.970, *df* = 1, $\rho > .05$; ϕ = .048). As with felony level offenses, the strength of associations between recidivism of domestic violence and prior criminal court involvement for statistically significant misdemeanor offenses are weak (see Table 20).

Table 19. Differences Between Domestic Violence Recidivists and Non-Recidivists on Prior Criminal Court Involvement for Felony Offenses: Bivariate Analysis (Chi-square Test)

Variable	Recidivists		Non-Recidivists		Total		χ^2
	n	%	*n*	%	*n*	%	
Prior DV [a] related felony offenses:							
Against persons							2.322
Involvement	8	4.3	9	2.1	17	2.8	
No involvement	176	95.7	414	97.9	590	97.2	
Total	184	100.0	423	100.0	607	100.0	
Against property							6.931**
Involvement	3	1.6	0	0	3	.5	
No involvement	181	98.4	423	100.0	604	99.5	
Total	184	100.0	423	100.0	607	100.0	
Deadly weapon used							.780
Involvement	2	1.1	9	2.1	11	1.8	
No involvement	182	98.9	414	97.9	596	98.2	
Total	184	100.0	423	100.0	607	100.0	
Prior non-DV felony offenses:							
Against persons							1.055
Involvement	21	11.4	37	8.7	58	9.6	
No involvement	163	88.6	386	91.3	549	90.4	
Total	184	100.0	423	100.0	607	100.0	
Prior non-DV felony offenses:							
Against property							6.430*
Involvement	42	22.8	61	14.4	103	17.0	
No involvement	142	77.2	362	85.6	504	83.0	
Total	184	100.0	423	100.0	607	100.0	

Table 19. Differences Between Domestic Violence Recidivists and Non-Recidivists on Prior Criminal Court Involvement for Felony Offenses: Bivariate Analysis (Chi-square Test) (Continued)

	Recidivists		Non-Recidivists		Total		χ^2
Variable	n	%	n	%	n	%	
Deadly weapon used							1.508
Involvement	21	11.4	35	8.3	56	9.2	
No involvement	163	88.6	388	91.7	551	90.8	
Total	184	100.0	423	100.0	607	100.0	
Against public administration							7.773**
Involvement	13	7.1	10	2.4	23	3.8	
No involvement	171	92.9	413	97.6	584	96.2	
Total	184	100.0	423	100.0	607	100.0	
Unlawful weapons							.739
Involvement	2	1.1	2	.5	4	.7	
No involvement	182	98.9	421	99.5	603	99.3	
Total	184	100.0	423	100.0	607	100.0	
Drugs							.418
Involvement	14	7.6	39	9.2	53	8.7	
No involvement	170	92.4	384	90.8	554	91.3	
Total	184	100.0	423	100.0	607	100.0	
Alcohol							.049
Involvement	3	1.6	8	1.9	11	1.8	
No involvement	181	98.4	415	98.1	596	98.2	
Total	184	100.0	423	100.0	607	100.0	

Note: Categories are not mutually exclusive; some men were involved with the courts for more than one type of criminal case. Of the sample of 607 men, none was involved with the courts for prior domestic violence related felony offenses related to public administration, public order, unlawful weapons, drugs, or alcohol, or non-domestic violence related felony offenses related to public order. The table does not include these categories.

[a] DV = Domestic Violence

$*p \leq .05.$ $**p \leq .01.$

Table 20. Differences Between Domestic Violence Recidivists and Non-Recidivists on Prior Criminal Court Involvement for Misdemeanor Offenses: Bivariate Analysis (Chi-square Test)

Variable	Recidivists		Non-Recidivists		Total		χ^2
	n	%	*n*	%	*n*	%	
Court involvement for DV[a] related offenses							11.946***
Involvement	21	11.4	17	4.0	38	6.3	
No involvement	163	88.6	406	96.0	569	93.7	
Total	184	100.0	423	100.0	607	100.0	
Court involvement for non-DV related offenses							2.970
Involvement	101	54.9	200	47.3	301	49.6	
No involvement	83	45.1	223	52.7	306	50.4	
Total	184	100.0	423	100.0	607	100.0	
Prior court involvement for any misdemeanor offenses							5.375*
Involvement	108	58.7	205	48.5	313	51.6	
No involvement	76	41.3	218	51.5	294	48.4	
Total	184	100.0	423	100.0	607	100.0	

Note: Categories are not mutually exclusive; some men were involved with the courts for more than one type of criminal case.
[a]DV = Domestic Violence
*$p \leq .05$. ***$p \leq .001$

Compared to non-recidivists, recidivists are more likely to have prior court involvement for misdemeanor domestic violence related offenses. A highly significant relationship exists between court involvement for domestic violence related offenses and recidivism ($\chi^2 = 11.946$, $df = 1$, $p \leq .001$; $\varphi = .140$). Approximately 11.4% of recidivists had prior involvement with the court for domestic violence related misdemeanor offenses, compared to 4.0% of non-recidivists, a difference of 7.4%. The measure of association indicates that the strength of the relationship is weak. As with prior court involvement for felony offenses, the relationship between criminal court involvement for misdemeanor offenses prior to the index case is statistically significant, but the strength of the association is very weak (χ^2 = 5.375, df = 1, $\rho \leq .05$; φ = .094). About 54.9% of the recidivists were involved with the courts for misdemeanor offenses prior to the index case compared to 47.3% of the non-recidivists, a difference of 7.6 percentage points.

Significant differences exist between recidivists and non-recidivists on prior criminal court involvement for misdemeanor offenses for both domestic violence and non-domestic violence related offenses against persons (see Table 21). No statistically significant differences exist between recidivists and non-recidivists on prior court involvement for domestic violence related misdemeanor offenses such as: against property (χ^2 = .452, df = 1, $\rho > .05$; φ = .027); against public administration (χ^2 = 1.886, df = 1, $\rho > .05$; φ = .056); and against public order (χ^2 = .368, df = 1, $\rho > .05$; φ = .025).

Table 21. Differences Between Domestic Violence Recidivists and Non-Recidivists on Prior Criminal Court Involvement for Misdemeanor Offenses: Bivariate Analysis (Chi-square Test)

Variable	Recidivists		Non-Recidivists		Total		χ^2
	n	%	n	%	n	%	
Prior DV[a] related misdemeanor offenses							
Against persons							14.260***
Involvement	17	9.2	10	2.4	27	4.4	
No involvement	167	90.8	413	97.6	580	95.6	
Total	184	100.0	423	100.0	607	100.0	
Against property							.452
Involvement	4	2.2	6	1.4	10	1.6	
No involvement	180	97.8	417	98.6	597	98.4	
Total	184	100.0	423	100.0	607	100.0	
Against public administration							1.886
Involvement	2	1.1	1	.2	3	.5	
No involvement	182	98.9	422	99.8	604	99.5	
Total	184	100.0	423	100.0	607	100.0	

Table 21. Differences Between Domestic Violence Recidivists and Non-Recidivists on Prior Criminal Court Involvement for Misdemeanor Offenses: Bivariate Analysis (Chi-square Test) (Continued)

Variable	Recidivists		Non-Recidivists		Total		χ^2
	n	%	*n*	%	*n*	%	
Against public order							.368
Involvement	1	.5	1	.2	2	.3	
No involvement	183	99.5	422	99.8	605	99.7	
Total	184	100.0	423	100.0	607	100.0	
Prior non-DV misdemeanor offenses							
Against persons							5.201*
Involvement	48	26.1	76	18.0	124	20.4	
No involvement	136	73.9	347	82.0	483	79.6	
Total	184	100.0	423	100.0	607	100.0	
Against property							.175
Involvement	33	17.9	70	16.5	103	17.0	
No involvement	151	82.1	353	83.5	504	83.0	
Total	184	100.0	423	100.0	607	100.0	
Against public administration							2.007
Involvement	25	13.6	41	9.7	66	10.9	
No involvement	159	86.4	382	90.3	541	89.1	
Total	184	100.0	423	100.0	607	100.0	
Against public order							.205
Involvement	6	3.3	11	2.6	17	2.8	
No involvement	178	96.7	412	97.4	590	97.2	
Total	184	100.0	423	100.0	607	100.0	

Table 21. Differences Between Domestic Violence Recidivists and Non-Recidivists on Prior Criminal Court Involvement for Misdemeanor Offenses: Bivariate Analysis (Chi-square Test) (Continued)

Variable	Recidivists		Non-Recidivists		Total		χ^2
	n		*n*		*n*		
Prior non-DV misdemeanor offenses (continued)							
Unlawful weapons							.001
Involvement	11	6.0	25	5.9	36	5.9	
No involvement	173	94.0	398	94.1	571	94.1	
Total	184	100.0	423	100.0	607	100.0	
Drugs							.194
Involvement	25	13.6	52	12.3	77	12.7	
No involvement	159	86.4	371	87.7	530	87.3	
Total	184	100.0	423	100.0	607	100.0	
Alcohol							.498
Involvement	24	13.0	54	12.8	78	12.9	
No involvement	160	87.0	369	87.2	529	87.1	
Total	184	100.0	423	100.0	607	100.0	

Note: Categories are not mutually exclusive; some men were involved with the courts for more than one type of criminal case. None of the 607 men in the sample were involved with the courts for prior domestic violence related misdemeanor offenses such as unlawful weapons, drugs, or alcohol. The table does not include these categories.
[a]DV = Domestic Violence
$*p \le .05. ***p \le .001.$

Additionally, no significant differences exist between recidivists and non-recidivists on prior court involvement for non-domestic violence related misdemeanor offenses such as: against property ($\chi^2 = .175$, $df = 1$, $\rho > .05$; $\varphi = .017$); against public administration ($\chi^2 = 2.007$, $df = 1$, $\rho > .05$; $\varphi = .057$); against public order ($\chi^2 = .205$, $df = 1$, $\rho > .05$; $\varphi = .018$); possession of unlawful weapons ($\chi^2 = .001$, $df = 1$, $\rho > .05$; $\varphi = .001$); drug related offenses ($\chi^2 = .194$, $df = 1$, $\rho > .05$; $\varphi = .018$); and alcohol related offenses ($\chi^2 = .009$, $df = 1$, $\rho > .05$; $\varphi = .004$).

Compared with non-recidivists, recidivists are more likely to be involved with the criminal courts for prior misdemeanor domestic violence related offenses against persons ($\chi^2 = 14.260$, $df = 1$, $\rho \leq .001$; $\varphi = .153$). Approximately 9.2% of recidivists were involved with the criminal courts for misdemeanor domestic violence related offenses against persons compared to 2.4% of non-recidivists, a difference of 6.8 percentage points. As with other variables, the measure of association indicates that this relationship is weak. Recidivists are also more likely than non-recidivists to have prior involvement with the courts for non-domestic violence related misdemeanor offenses against persons ($\chi^2 = 5.201$, $df = 1$, $\rho \leq .05$; $\varphi = .093$).

Chi-Square Tests for Index Case Legal Sanctions and Recidivism

Legal sanctions for the index case include civil sanctions (protective orders), arrest, incarceration, probation, and revocation of probation. As shown in Table 22, no statistically significant relationship exists between incarceration for the index case and recidivism ($\chi^2 = 3.074$, $df = 1$, $\rho > .05$; $\varphi = .071$).

Despite statistically significant relationships between specific legal sanctions and recidivism, the strength of those relationships is very weak. For example, a significant relationship exists between civil sanctions for the index case and recidivism of domestic violence ($\chi^2 = 9.705$, $df = 1$, $\rho \leq .01$; $\varphi = .126$). About 60.3% of recidivists were involved with the civil courts for the index case compared to 46.6% of non-recidivists, a difference of 13.7 percentage points. The measure of association indicates that the strength of the relationship is weak. Additionally, a significant relationship exists between arrest for the index case and recidivism, and suggests that recidivists were less likely to have been arrested for the index case ($\chi^2 = 7.183$, $df = 1$, $\rho \leq .01$; $\varphi = .109$). Compared to 59.6% of the non-recidivists, approximately 47.5% of the recidivists were arrested, a difference of 12.1 percentage points. The strength of the association between arrest and recidivism is extremely weak.

As Table 22 also illustrates, recidivists were less likely to be put on probation for the index case ($\chi^2 = 6.168$, $df = 1$, $\rho \leq .05$; $\varphi = .101$). About 42.9% of recidivists were on probation for the index case compared to 53.9% of non-recidivists, a difference of 11 percentage points. The measure of association for probation and recidivism indicates that the strength of the relationship is weak. The pattern of statistical significance with a weak association also holds for the relationship between revocation and recidivism ($\chi^2 = 5.925$, $df = 1$, $\rho \leq .05$; $\varphi = .099$).

Table 22. Differences Between Recidivists and Non-Recidivists on Legal Sanctions for Index Case: Bivariate Analysis (Chi-square Test)

Variable	Recidivists		Non-Recidivists		Total		χ^2
	n	%[a]	n	%[a]	n	%[a]	
Civil Sanctions for Index Case[b]							9.705**
Protective Order	111	60.3	197	46.6	308	50.7	
No Protective Order	73	39.7	226	53.4	299	49.3	
Total	184	100.0	423	100.0	607	100.0	
Arrest for Index Case[b]							7.183**
Arrest	88	47.5	252	59.6	340	56.0	
No Arrest	96	52.2	171	40.4	267	44.0	
Total	184	99.7	423	100.0	607	100.0	
Incarcerated in Jail for Index Case[b]							3.074
Incarcerated	40	21.7	67	15.8	107	17.6	
Not incarcerated	144	78.3	356	84.2	500	82.4	
Total	184	100.0	423	100.0	607	100.0	
Probation for Index Case[b]							6.168*
Probation	79	42.9	228	53.9	307	50.6	
No Probation	105	57.1	195	46.1	300	49.4	
Total	184	100.0	423	100.0	607	100.0	
Revocation of Probation for Index Case[b]							5.925*
Revocation	46	25.0	70	16.5	116	19.1	
No revocation	138	75.0	353	81.1	491	80.9	
Total	184	100.0	423	97.6	607	100.0	

[a] *Note*: Percentages may not sum to 100% due to rounding.
[b] Categories are not mutually exclusive; some men received more than one legal sanction for the index case.
*$p \leq .05$ **$p \leq .01$ ***$p \leq .001$

Chi-Square Tests for the Legal Sanctions Dose-Response Index and Recidivism

The Legal Sanctions Dose-Response Index captures the cumulative effects of legal sanctions (or dose-responses) for the index case. As illustrated in Table 23, no statistically significant relationship exists between men who experienced three legal sanctions and recidivism (χ^2 = 1.807, df = 1, ρ > .05; φ = .055). The strongest statistically significant relationship is between men who experienced two legal sanctions (typically arrest and probation) and recidivism (χ^2 = 26.287, df = 1, $\rho \leq$ .001; φ = .208). Non-recidivists were over twice as likely as recidivist to experience two sanctions. More specifically, about 17.4% of recidivists experienced two sanctions, compared to 38.5% of non-recidivists, a difference of 21.1 percentage points. The measure of association indicates that the strength of the relationship is weak. In contrast, a significant relationship exists between receiving one sanction (typically a protective order) and recidivism, suggesting that compared to non-recidivists, recidivists were more like to have received only one legal sanction (χ^2 = 6.675, df = 1, $\rho \leq$ .01; φ = .105). Approximately 52.7% of recidivists experienced one legal sanction for the index case compared to 41.4% of non-recidivists, a difference of 11.3 percentage points. Finally, a significant relationship exists between four to five sanctions and recidivism (χ^2 = 4.334, df = 1, $\rho \leq$ .05; φ = .084). The measures of association for one sanction and recidivism, and four to five sanctions and recidivism indicate that the strength of these relationships are also weak.

Chi-Square Tests for Battering Intervention Program Participation and Recidivism

Although all in the sample of 607 men were court ordered to attend a battering intervention program, participation was low for both recidivists and non-recidivists (see Table 24). A significant relationship exists between not participating in a battering intervention program and recidivism of domestic violence related offenses (χ^2 = 5.113, df = 1, $\rho \leq$ .05; φ = .092). Approximately 66.3% of recidivists had no contact with a battering intervention program, compared to 56.5% of non-recidivists, a difference of 9.8 percentage points. Although the relationship between not contacting a battering intervention program and recidivism is statistically significant at the .05 level, the association is weak. In general, of the men in the sample who participated in a battering intervention program, recidivists were less likely to have completed the program than were non-recidivists.

Table 23. Differences Between Recidivists and Non-Recidivists on the Legal Sanctions Dose-Response Index: Bivariate Analysis (Chi-square Test)

Variable	Recidivists		Non-Recidivists		Total		χ^2
	n	%[a]	n	%[a]	n	%[a]	
One legal sanction	97	52.7	175	41.4	272	44.8	6.675**
Two legal sanctions	32	17.4	163	38.5	195	32.1	26.287***
Three legal sanctions	19	10.3	30	7.1	49	8.1	1.807
Four to five legal sanctions	36	19.6	55	13.0	91	15.0	4.334*
Total	184	100.0	423	100.0	607	100.0	

[a] *Note*: Percentages may not sum to 100% due to rounding.
*$p \leq .05$ **$p \leq .01$ ***$p \leq .001$

Table 24. Differences Between Recidivists and Non-Recidivists on Battering Intervention Program Participation: Bivariate Analysis (Chi-square Test)

Variable	Recidivists		Non-Recidivists		Total		χ^2
	n	%[a]	n	%[a]	n	%[a]	
No contact with program	122	66.3	239	56.5	361	59.5	5.113*
Terminated from program	28	15.2	48	11.3	76	12.5	1.753
Completed program	34	18.5	136	32.2	170	28.0	11.889***
Total	184	100.0	423	100.0	607	100.0	

[a] *Note*: Percentages may not sum to 100% due to rounding.
*$p \leq .05$ **$p \leq .01$ ***$p \leq .001$

A significant relationship exists between completion of a battering intervention program and recidivism ($\chi^2 = 11.889$, $df = 1$, $\rho \leq .001$; $\varphi = .140$). Approximately 18.5% of the recidivists in the sample completed a battering intervention program compared to 32.2% of non-recidivists who completed a battering intervention program, a difference of 13.7

percentage points. Whereas the relationship between completion of a battering intervention program and recidivism is significant at the 0.001 level, the association is weak.

With a completion rate of 28%, the factors that characterize low participation and completion of court-ordered battering intervention warrant closer examination. For the purposes of this particular analysis, there are two subgroups: completers and non-completers. The group of completers consists of men who attended all required 36 hours of battering intervention. The group of non-completers consists of men who did not contact a program and men terminated from the program. Comparing program non-completers to completers, the additional analyses indicate that the characteristics of recidivists who do not complete the battering intervention program were comparable and similar to recidivists in the overall sample on most measures.

The t-test for independent samples compares the means between recidivists who did not complete a battering intervention program and recidivists who did complete a program. Recidivists who did not complete a program and recidivists in the overall sample differ in the results of the t-test for the means of age (which was significant for the overall sample) and months on probation (which was not significant in the overall sample). For example, unlike recidivists in the overall sample of men, the results of the comparisons of the means for age were not statistically significant when comparing recidivists who did not complete a program versus those who did complete ($t = 1.242$, $\rho > .05$, $g = -.235$). Unlike recidivists in the overall sample, the results of the comparisons of the means for months on probation are statistically significant when comparing recidivists who completed a battering intervention program and those who did not. Recidivists who were also non-completers spent less time on probation ($t = 2.473$, $\rho \leq .05$, $g = -.468$). According to the measure of association, the effect size for months spent on probation is moderate. Like recidivists in the overall sample, the results of the comparisons of means indicate that the time served in jail for the index case is not statistically significant ($t = -1.013$, $\rho > .05$, $g = .191$). Compared to recidivists who completed a battering intervention program, recidivists who did not complete spent more years incarcerated during the follow-up period ($t = 3.229$, $\rho \leq$

.001, g = .611). According to the measure of association, the effect size
for years incarcerated during the follow-up period is moderate.

Bivariate analyses conducted to examine differences between
recidivists who did not complete a battering intervention program and
those who completed a program parallel the results of the bivariate
analyses for the entire sample. For example, recidivists in the overall
sample were more likely to be Black men; similarly, recidivists who
did not complete the program were more likely to be Black men (χ^2 =
7.623, df = 1, φ = .204, $\rho \leq$ .001). Just as recidivists in general were less
likely to be arrested for the index offense, recidivists who did not
complete the battering intervention program were less likely to be
arrested (χ^2 = 8.660, df = 1, φ = .154, $\rho \leq$ .001) and, therefore, less
likely to be on probation (χ^2 = 10.396, df = 1, φ = .217, $\rho \leq$ .001). As
with the overall sample of men who recidivated, recidivists who did not
complete a battering intervention program were more likely to have
come to the attention of the courts through a civil protective order for
the index case. Recidivists who did not complete the program were also
more likely to be involved with the criminal courts (not civil courts) for
domestic violence related offenses after the index case (χ^2 = 7.872, df =
1, φ = .207, $\rho \leq$ .01). As with the overall sample, the measures of
association indicate that the relationships are weak. Because the
subgroup of recidivists who did not complete the battering intervention
program generally mirrors the overall group of recidivists, additional
analysis was not conducted.

Chi-Square Tests for Post-Index Case Non-Domestic Violence Related Offenses and Recidivism

During the follow-up period, 45.6% of the 607 men in the sample were
involved with the criminal courts for either domestic violence related
offenses, non-domestic violence related offenses, or both. Civil and
criminal court involvement for domestic violence related offenses
committed during the follow-up period are intrinsic to the definition of
recidivism. Thus, Table 25 presents only comparisons between
recidivists and non-recidivists for criminal court involvement for non-
domestic violence related offenses.

A significant relationship exists between post-index non-domestic
violence related offenses and recidivism. The likelihood of being
involved with the courts for non-domestic violence related offenses
during the follow-up period is greater for recidivists than it is for non-

recidivists ($\chi2$ = 39.237, df = 1, $\rho \le$ .001; φ = .254). Over half (51.6%) of recidivists were involved with the criminal courts during the follow-up period compared to 25.5% of the non-recidivists, a difference of 26.1 percentage points. The measure of association indicates that the strength of the relationship between being involved with the courts after the index case for non-domestic violence related offenses and recidivism of domestic violence is weak.

Table 25. Differences Between Recidivists and Non-Recidivists on Post-Index Case Non-Domestic Violence Related Offense Court Involvement: Bivariate Analysis (Chi-square Test)

Variable	Recidivists		Non-Recidivists		Total		χ^2
	n	%[a]	*n*	%[a]	*n*	%[a]	
Post-Index Non-Domestic Violence Related Offenses							
Criminal							39.237**
Court involvement	95	51.6	108	25.5	203	33.4	
No court involvement	89	48.4	315	74.5	404	66.6	
Total	184	100.0	423	100.0	607	100.0	

[a] *Note*: Percentages may not sum to 100% due to rounding.

Chi-Square Tests for Post-Index Case Criminal Court Involvement for Felony Offenses and Recidivism

As shown in Table 26, a significant relationship exists between post-index case court involvement for non-domestic violence related felony offenses and recidivism.

The likelihood of being involved with the courts for non-domestic violence related felony offenses during the follow-up period is greater for recidivists than it is for non-recidivists (χ^2 = 38.760, *df* = 1, $\rho \le$ .001; φ = .253). Over one-third (38.6%) of recidivists were involved with the courts for non-domestic violence related felony offenses after the index case compared with 15.6% of non-recidivists, a difference of 23 percentage points. The measure of association indicates that the strength of the relationship between post-index case court involvements for non-domestic violence related felony offenses and recidivism of domestic violence is weak.

Table 26. Differences Between Domestic Violence Recidivists and Non-Recidivists on Post-Index Criminal Court Involvement for Felony Offenses: Bivariate Analysis (Chi-square Test)

Variable	Recidivists		Non-Recidivists		Total		χ^2
	n	%	*n*	%	*n*	%	
Domestic violence related only							
Involvement	90	48.9	0	0	90	14.8	
No involvement	94	51.1	423	100.0	517	85.2	
Total	184	100.0	423	100.0	607	100.0	
							38.760***
Non-domestic violence related only							
Involvement	71	38.6	66	15.1	137	22.6	
No involvement	113	61.4	357	84.4	470	77.4	
Total	184	100.0	423	100.0	607	100.0	
Court involvement for any felony							
Involvement	130	70.7	66	15.6	196	32.3	
No involvement	54	29.3	357	84.4	411	67.7	
Total	184	100.0	423	100.0	607	100.0	

Note: Categories are not mutually exclusive; some men were involved with the courts for more than one type of criminal case.
***$p \leq .001$.

Significant differences exist between recidivists and non-recidivists on post-index case court involvement for non-domestic violence related felony offenses against property, use of a deadly weapon, against public administration, carrying unlawful weapons, and drug offenses (see Table 27). No apparent significant difference exists between recidivists and non-recidivists on court involvement after the index case for non-domestic violence related felony offenses against persons ($\chi^2 = 3.227$, $df = 1$, $p > .05$; $\varphi = .073$) and alcohol related offenses ($\chi^2 = .000$, $df = 1$, $p > .05$; $\varphi = .001$).

Table 27. Differences Between Domestic Violence Recidivists and Non-Recidivists on Post-Index Case Criminal Court Involvement for Felony Offenses: Bivariate Analysis (Chi-square Test)

Variable	Recidivists		Non-Recidivists		Total		χ^2
	n	%	*n*	%	*n*	%	
Post-index DV[a] felony offenses							
Against persons							
Involvement	83	45.1	0	0	83	13.7	
No involvement	101	54.9	423	100.0	524	86.3	
Total	184	100.0	423	100.0	607	100.0	
Against property							
Involvement	2	1.1	0	0	2	.3	
No involvement	182	98.9	423	100.0	605	99.7	
Total	184	100.0	423	100.0	607	100.0	
Deadly weapon used							
Involvement	9	4.9	0	0	9	1.5	
No involvement	175	95.1	423	100.0	598	98.5	
Total	184	100.0	423	100.0	607	100.0	
Post-index non-DV felony offenses							3.227
Against persons							
Involvement	12	6.5	14	3.3	26	4.3	
No involvement	172	93.5	409	96.7	581	95.7	
Total	184	100.0	423	100.0	607	100.0	
Post-index non-DV felony offenses (continued)							
Against property							11.694***
Involvement	25	13.6	23	5.4	48	7.9	
No involvement	159	86.4	400	94.6	559	92.1	
Total	184	100.0	423	100.0	607	100.0	

Table 27. Differences Between Domestic Violence Recidivists and Non-Recidivists on Post-Index Case Criminal Court Involvement for Felony Offenses: Bivariate Analysis (Chi-square Test) (Continued)

Variable	Recidivists		Non-Recidivists		Total		χ^2
	n	%	n	%	n	%	
Deadly weapon used							19.476***
Involvement	18	9.8	8	1.9	26	4.3	
No involvement	166	90.2	415	98.1	581	95.7	
Total	184	100.0	423	100.0	607	100.0	
Against public administration							4.652*
Involvement	14	7.6	15	3.5	29	4.8	
No involvement	170	92.4	408	96.5	578	95.2	
Total	184	100.0	423	100.0	607	100.0	
Unlawful weapons							4.613*
Involvement	2	1.1	0	0	2	.3	
No involvement	182	98.9	423	100.0	605	99.7	
Total	184	100.0	423	100.0	607	100.0	
Post-index non-DV felony offenses (continued)							
Drugs							4.951*
Involvement	18	9.8	21	5.0	39	6.4	
No involvement	166	90.2	402	95.0	568	93.6	
Total	184	100.0	423	100.0	607	100.0	
Alcohol							.000
Involvement	3	1.6	7	1.7	10	1.6	
No involvement	181	98.4	416	98.3	597	98.4	
Total	184	100.0	423	100.0	607	100.0	

Note: Categories are not mutually exclusive; some men were involved with the courts for more than one type of criminal case. Of the sample of 607 men, none was involved with the courts for post-index non-domestic violence related felony offenses related to public order. The table does not include this category.
[a]DV = Domestic Violence
*$p \leq .05$. **$p \leq .01$. ***$p \leq .001$.

Statistically significant relationships exist between post-index court involvement for non-domestic violence related felony offenses against property and recidivism, and between use of a deadly weapon and recidivism. The likelihood of involvement with the courts for non-domestic violence related offenses against property during the follow-up period is greater for recidivists than it is for non-recidivists (χ^2 = 11.694, df = 1, $\rho \leq .001$; φ = .139). Approximately 13.6% of recidivists were involved with the courts for non-domestic violence felony offenses compared to 5.4% of non-recidivists, a difference of 8.2 percentage points. The strength of the relationship is weak, according to the measure of association.

Court involvement for use of a deadly weapon was highly significant for recidivists compared to non-recidivists (χ^2 = 19.476, df = 1, $\rho \leq .001$; φ = .179). About 9.8% of recidivists were involved with the criminal courts for felony use of a deadly weapon compared with 1.9% of non-recidivists, a difference of 7.9 percentage points. Despite the statistical significance, however, the strength of the relationship is weak, according to the measure of association.

Significant relationships exist between the independent variables for court involvement for felony offenses against public administration, carrying unlawful weapons, and drug offenses and the dependent variable recidivism. Compared with non-recidivists, recidivists were more likely to be involved with the criminal courts for felony offenses against public administration (χ^2 = 4.652, df = 1, $\rho \leq .05$; φ = .088), carrying unlawful weapons (χ^2 = 4.613, df = 1, $\rho \leq .05$; φ = .087), and drugs (χ^2 = 4.951, df = 1, $\rho \leq .05$; φ = .090). The measure of association indicates that the strength of the relationships between court involvement for these offenses and recidivism is very weak.

Chi-Square Tests of Post-Index Case Criminal Court Involvement for Misdemeanor Offenses and Recidivism

A significant relationship exists between court involvement for non-domestic violence related misdemeanor offenses and recidivism during the follow-up period (see Table 28). The likelihood of being involved with the courts for non-domestic violence related misdemeanor offenses during the follow-up period is greater for recidivists than it is for non-recidivists (χ^2 = 17.147, df = 1, $\rho \leq .001$; φ = .168). Almost one-third (32.1%) of recidivists were involved with the courts for non-domestic violence related misdemeanor offenses after the index case compared with 17% of non-recidivists, a difference of 15.1 percentage points.

Table 28. Differences Between Domestic Violence Recidivists and Non-Recidivists on Post-Index Criminal Court Involvement for Misdemeanor Offenses: Bivariate Analysis (Chi-square Test)

Variable	Recidivists		Non-Recidivists		Total		χ^2
	n	%	*n*	%	*n*	%	
DV[a] related only							
Involvement	89	48.4	0	0	89	14.7	
No involvement	95	51.6	423	100.0	518	85.3	
Total	427	107.4	423	100.0	607	100.0	
Non-DV related only							17.147***
Involvement	59	32.1	72	17.0	131	21.6	
No involvement	125	67.9	351	83.0	476	78.4	
Total	184	100.0	423	100.0	607	100.0	
Combined DV and non-DV							
Involvement	116	63.0	72	17.0	188	31.0	
No involvement	68	37.0	351	83.0	419	69.0	
Total	184	100.0	423	100.0	607	100.0	

Note: Categories are not mutually exclusive; some men were involved with the courts for more than one type of criminal case.
[a]DV = Domestic Violence
***$p \leq .001$

The measure of association indicates that the strength of the relationship between post-index case court involvements for non-domestic violence related felony offenses and recidivism of domestic violence is weak.

Significant differences exist between recidivists and non-recidivists on post-index case criminal court involvement for misdemeanor offenses for non-domestic violence related offenses against persons, offenses against public administration, and carrying unlawful weapons (see Table 29). There are no statistically significant differences between recidivists and non-recidivists on post-index case involvement for misdemeanor offenses such as: offenses against property (χ^2 = 3.361, df = 1, ρ > .05; φ = .074); offenses against public order (χ^2 = 2.756, df = 1, ρ > .05; φ = .067); drug related offenses (χ^2 = 3.403, df = 1, ρ > .05; φ = .065); and alcohol related offenses (χ^2 = .000, df = 1, ρ > .05; φ = .001).

A statistically significant relationship exists between court involvement for misdemeanor offenses against persons and recidivism (χ^2 = 19.784, df = 1, $\rho \le$ .001; φ = .181). During the follow-up period, approximately 7.6% of recidivists were involved with the courts for non-domestic violence offenses against persons compared to .9% of non-recidivists, a difference of 6.7 percentage points. The measure of association indicates that the strength of the relationship is weak. Compared with non-recidivists, recidivists are more likely to be involved with the criminal courts during the follow-up period for misdemeanor non-domestic violence related offenses against public administration (χ^2 = 6.397, df = 1, $\rho \le$ .05; φ = .088), and misdemeanor offenses for carrying unlawful weapons (χ^2 = 3.976, df = 1, $\rho \le$ .05; φ = .087). As with other variables, the measure of association indicates that the strength of the relationship is very weak.

Table 29. Differences Between Domestic Violence Recidivists and Non-Recidivists on Post-Index Case Criminal Court Involvement for Misdemeanor Offenses: Bivariate Analysis (Chi-square Test)

Variable	Recidivists		Non-Recidivists		Total		χ^2
	n	%	n	%	n	%	
Post-index DV[a] misdemeanor offenses							
Against persons							
Involvement	89	48.4	0	0	89	14.7	
No involvement	95	51.6	423	100.0	518	85.3	
Total	184	100.0	423	100.0	607	100.0	
Against property							
Involvement	1	.5	0	0	1	.2	
No involvement	183	99.5	423	100.0	606	99.8	
Total	184	100.0	423	100.0	607	100.0	

Table 29. Differences Between Domestic Violence Recidivists and Non-Recidivists on Post-Index Case Criminal Court Involvement for Misdemeanor Offenses: Bivariate Analysis (Chi-square Test) (Continued)

Variable	Recidivists		Non-Recidivists		Total		χ^2
	n	%	*n*	%	*n*	%	
Post-index non-DV misdemeanor offenses							
Against persons							19.784***
Involvement	14	7.6	4	.9	18	3.0	
No involvement	170	92.4	419	99.1	589	97.0	
Total	184	100.0	423	100.0	607	100.0	
Against property							3.361
Involvement	18	9.8	24	5.7	42	6.9	
No involvement	166	90.58	399	94.3	565	93.1	
Total	184	100.0	423	100.0	607	100.0	
Post-index non-DV misdemeanor offenses							
Against public administration							6.397*
Involvement	20	10.9	22	5.2	42	6.9	
No involvement	164	89.1	401	94.8	565	93.1	
Total	184	100.0	423	100.0	607	100.0	
Against public order							2.756
Involvement	5	2.7	4	.9	9	1.5	
No involvement	179	97.3	419	99.1	598	98.5	
Total	184	100.0	423	100.0	607	100.0	
Unlawful weapons							3.976*
Involvement	5	2.7	3	.7	8	1.3	
No involvement	179	97.3	420	99.3	599	98.7	
Total	184	100.0	423	100.0	607	100.0	
Drugs							3.403
Involvement	9	5.0	9	2.1	18	3.0	
No involvement	175	95.1	414	97.9	589	97.0	
Total	184	100.0	423	100.0	607	100.0	

Table 29. Differences Between Domestic Violence Recidivists and Non-Recidivists on Post-Index Case Criminal Court Involvement for Misdemeanor Offenses: Bivariate Analysis (Chi-square Test) (continued)

Variable	Recidivists		Non-Recidivists		Total		χ^2
	n	%	n	%	n	%	
Post-index non-DV misdemeanor offenses (continued)							
Alcohol							.000
Involvement	7	3.8	16	3.8	23	3.8	
No involvement	177	96.2	407	96.2	584	96.2	
Total	184	100.0	423	100.0	607	100.0	

Note: Categories are not mutually exclusive; some men were involved with the courts for more than one type of criminal case. Of the sample of 607 men, none was involved with the courts for post-index domestic violence related misdemeanor offenses related to public administration or public order. The table does not include these categories.

[a]DV = Domestic Violence

*$p \leq .05$.

Chi-Square Tests for Post-Index Case Incarceration in Jail or Prison and Recidivism

As shown in Table 30, a significant relationship exists between incarceration in jail or prison for any length of time during the follow-up period and recidivism ($\chi^2 = 53.376$, $df = 1$, $p \leq .001$; $\varphi = .297$, $p \leq .001$). Approximately 66.3% of the recidivists were incarcerated in either jail or prison during the follow-up period compared to 34.3% of the non-recidivists, a difference of 32 percentage points. This is not surprising as many of the recidivists were involved with the criminal courts for domestic and non-domestic violence related offenses during the follow-up period. The measure of association indicates a moderate relationship exists between incarceration during the follow-up period and recidivism of domestic violence related offenses.

Table 30. Differences Between Recidivists and Non-Recidivists on Post-Index Case Incarceration: Bivariate Analysis (Chi-square Test)

Variable	Recidivists		Non-Recidivists		Total		χ^2
	n	%[a]	n	%[a]	n	%[a]	
Incarcerated in jail or prison anytime during five-year follow-up period							53.376***
Incarcerated	122	66.3	145	34.3	267	44.0	
Not incarcerated	62	33.7	278	65.7	340	56.0	
Total	184	100.0	423	100.0	607	100.0	

[a] *Note*: Percentages may not sum to 100% due to rounding.

[b] Categories are not mutually exclusive; some men were involved with the courts for more than one type of case.

*$p \le .05$ **$p \le .01$ ***$p \le .001$

Cox Proportional Hazards Regression Models of Predictors of Recidivism of Domestic Violence

The results of three Cox proportional hazards regression models are presented in Table 31. The models demonstrate the hazard ratio or risk for recidivism during the follow-up period, focusing on the time that elapses until recidivism (in years). The hazard ratio is the exponentiated value of each regression coefficient and the relative risk of the covariate to its reference group (McCarroll et al., 2000). Hazard ratios less than 1.0 indicate that the greater the covariate, the less the hazard or relative risk; hazard ratios greater than 1.0 indicate that the greater the covariate, the greater the hazard or relative risk (Garson, 2008a).

Model 1 is limited to demographic covariates (age and race/ethnicity), prior civil court involvement for protective orders, and prior criminal court involvement for domestic violence related and non-domestic violence related offenses. This model indicates that, if these are the only covariates considered, age, race/ethnicity, prior civil court involvement for protective orders, and prior court involvement for non-domestic violence related offenses are not statistically significant. A statistically significant positive risk ratio exists for recidivism of domestic violence for men with prior involvement with the criminal courts for domestic violence related offenses. To summarize Model 1, for men in the sample with prior criminal court involvement for domestic violence related offenses (versus those with no such prior involvement), the relative risk of recidivism is higher by a factor of 1.588, or 58.8%, holding all other covariates constant (B = .463, SE = .222, $p \leq .05$).

Model 2 extends Model 1 by including the covariates for the Legal Sanctions Dose-Response Index. As in Model 1, the covariates age, race/ethnicity, prior civil court involvement for protective orders, and prior criminal court involvement for non-domestic violence related offenses are not statistically significant. Two covariates are statistically significant. As in Model 1, the risk ratio is higher for men with prior criminal court involvement for domestic violence related offenses (versus those with no such prior involvement) (B = .625, SE = .225, $p \leq .01$). In this model, the relative risk of recidivism is higher by a factor of 1.868, or 86.8%, holding all other covariates constant. Also statistically significant is the covariate for two legal sanctions for the index case. For men who received two (versus one) legal sanctions, the relative risk of recidivism is lower by a factor of .530, or 47.0%, holding all other covariates constant (B = -.635, SE = .217, $p \leq .01$).

In summary, the relative risk of recidivism is greater for men who have prior criminal court involvement for domestic violence related offenses (versus no involvement) and is less for men who have a "dose" of two (versus one) legal sanctions imposed upon them for the index case.

Finally, Model 3 expands the prior two models by including the covariates battering intervention program participation and incarceration for any offense during the follow-up period. As shown in Model 1 and Model 2, the covariates age, race/ethnicity, prior civil court involvement for protective orders, criminal court involvement for non-domestic violence offenses are not statistically significant. Additionally, the relative risk of recidivism is not statistically significant for men who have doses of three legal sanctions and four to five legal sanctions (versus one) imposed upon them for the index case.

Table 31. Cox Proportional Hazard Regressions Predicting the Risk of Recidivism for Male Perpetrators of Domestic Violence, 2001 (N = 607)

Covariates	Model 1 B (SE)	Model 1 HR	Model 1 95% CI	Model 2 B (SE)	Model 2 HR	Model 2 95% CI	Model 3 B (SE)	Model 3 HR	Model 3 95% CI
Age (Years)	.010 (.008)	1.01	[.994, 1.026]	.009 (.008)	1.009	[.993, 1.025]	.013 (.008)	1.013	[.997, 1.030]
Race/Ethnicity Black									
Hispanic	.354 (.197)	1.425	[.968, 2.099]	.358 (.196)	1.431	[.975, 2.099]	.350 (.199)	1.419	[.960, 2.096]
White	.112 (.188)	1.118	[.774, 1.615]	.111 (.189)	1.118	[.772, 1.619]	.074 (.191)	1.077	[.742, 1.565]
Prior Court Involvement									
Civil (Protective Order)	.361 (.221)	1.435	[.931, 2.211]	.364 (.217)	1.44	[.941, 2.201]	.414 (.221)	1.513	[.981, 2.33]
Criminal Court Domestic violence related	.463* (.222)	1.588	[1.028, 2.454]	.625** (.225)	1.868	[1.201, 2.906]	.504* (.238)	1.655	[1.038, 2.638]
Non-domestic violence related	-.011 (.175)	0.989	[.703, 1.393]	-.041 (.179)	0.96	[.676, 1.364]	-.121 (.183)	0.886	[.619, 1.268]

Table 31. Cox Proportional Hazard Regressions Predicting the Risk of Recidivism for Male Perpetrators of Domestic Violence, 2001 (N = 607) (continued)

Covariates	Model 1			Model 2			Model 3		
	B (SE)	HR	95% CI	B (SE)	HR	95% CI	B (SE)	HR	95% CI
Legal Sanctions Dose-Response Index									
One sanction									
Two sanctions				-.635** (.217)	0.53	[.346, .810]	-.584** (.235)	0.558	[.352, .884]
Three sanctions				-.249 (.272)	0.78	[.457, 1.330]	-.308 (.273)	0.735	[.430, 1.256]
Four to five sanctions				-.074 (.206)	0.929	[.620, 1.392]	-.098 (.212)	0.907	[.598, 1.375]
Battering Intervention									
No contact									
Terminated							-.066 (.227)	0.936	[.600, 1.459]
Completed							-.010 (.228)	0.99	[.634, 1.546]
Incarceration Post-Index Case (Years)							.129* (.052)	1.138	[1.028, 1.259]
-2 log likelihood	1553.409			1543.592			1537.171		
Overall χ^2	14.269			23.674			30.794		
Degrees of freedom	6			9			12		
ρ	< .05			< .01			< .01		

Note. CI = Confidence Interval; HR = Hazard Ratio. The HR is the antilog of the B. Standard errors are in parentheses. *p < .05. **p < .01.

The results for Model 3 indicate that three covariates have statistically significant risk ratios for recidivism of domestic violence related offenses: prior criminal court involvement for domestic violence related offenses, two legal sanctions imposed, and incarceration during the follow-up period. For men in the sample with criminal court involvement for domestic violence related offenses prior to the index case (versus those with no such prior offense), the relative risk of recidivism is higher by a factor of 1.655 or 65.5%, holding all other covariates constant (B = .504, SE = .238, $p \leq .05$). Additionally, for men in the sample who received two legal sanctions for the index case, the relative risk of recidivism is lower by a factor of .558, or 44.2% (relative to those with one legal sanction), holding all else constant (B = -.594, SE = .235, $p \leq .01$). Finally, for men in the sample who were incarcerated in jail or prison during the follow-up period, a one-year increase in time incarcerated is associated with a one unit increase in the hazard ratio for recidivism of 1.138, holding all other covariates constant (B = .129, S.E. = .052, $p \leq .05$). Because it has the greatest overall chi-square and the lowest -2 log likelihood, Model 3 is the better predictor model. The estimated survival curve uses Model 3 (see Figure 1). Note that the potential for multicollinearity exists in the multivariate model (i.e., incarceration as a result of recidivism could possibly affect the relationship between the covariate "Incarcerated during follow-up period" for any offense and the dependent variable "recidivism"). A bivariate regression model using the variables incarceration and recidivism was conducted. The positive relationship between the covariate and the dependent variable remains (B = $\leq .001$, SE $\leq .001, p \leq 01$).

The Cox survival curve predicts the likelihood of recidivism for the average individual in the sample (Case, 2008). Figure 1 graphically represents the number of years men in the sample maintained their non-recidivism status, stratified by the numbers of sanctions imposed for the index case.

To compare differences in the number of legal sanctions, all groups begin with a value of 100% survival rate. Men who received two legal sanctions (versus one) were more likely to maintain their non-recidivism status longer. No statistically significant difference exists between those who experienced more than three legal sanctions, or four to five legal sanctions, and the reference group of one legal sanction.

Figure 1: Post-Index Case Survival Curve by Legal Sanctions Dose-Response

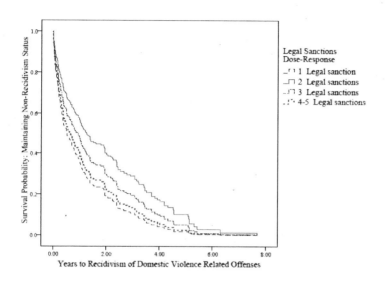

FINDINGS RELATED TO HYPOTHESES

This study uses a Cox regression analysis to test the hypotheses. Related to the hypotheses, the covariates expected to affect the hazard ratio or relative risk for recidivism during the follow-up period include the following: age; race/ethnicity, prior civil court involvement for protective orders, domestic violence related offenses, and non-domestic violence related offenses; completion of a battering intervention program; and legal sanctions as measured by the Legal Sanctions Dose-Response Index. As discussed in the previous section, three covariates were statistically significant. To introduce the results of the analysis, each hypothesis is listed below and followed by a brief discussion of the results. A discussion of the significant findings and their implications follows in Chapter Seven.

Age and recidivism of domestic violence

Hypothesis 1a states that the hazard ratio for recidivism for domestic violence related offenses is negatively related to age at the time of the index case offense. Despite a statistically significant relationship between age and recidivism found by the *t*-test analysis, the hypothesis is unsupported in the multivariate analysis; age is not a significant factor for the hazard ratio for recidivism.

Race /Ethnicity and Recidivism of Domestic Violence

Hypothesis 1b states that the relative risk of recidivism for domestic violence related offenses is not associated with race or ethnicity. Because Black men comprise the largest group in the sample, the regression model uses Black men as the reference group. However, as indicated by the Cox proportional hazard regression model, a relationship between race and recidivism does not exist for this sample of men and the multivariate analysis does not support Hypothesis 1b.

Prior Court Involvement and Recidivism of Domestic Violence

To examine the relationship between prior court involvement and recidivism of domestic violence related offenses, the analysis treats civil court involvement for protective orders, criminal court involvement for domestic violence related offenses, and criminal court involvement for non-domestic violence related offenses as discrete covariates. The categories are not mutually exclusive in that a man may have had court involvement for more than one type of offense prior to the index case.

Hypothesis 2a states that the relative risk of recidivism for domestic violence related offenses is greater for men with prior civil court involvement for protective orders than for men with no prior civil court involvement for protective orders. The results of the chi-square analysis indicate a significant relationship between prior civil court involvement for protective orders and recidivism. The Cox proportional hazard regression model, however, does not support Hypothesis 2a.

Hypothesis 2b states that the relative risk of recidivism for domestic violence related offenses is greater for men with prior criminal court involvement for domestic violence related offenses than for men with no prior criminal court involvement for domestic violence related offenses. The results of the Cox proportional hazard regression model demonstrate that prior criminal court involvement for domestic violence related offenses has a statistically significant positive relationship with the relative risk of recidivism. In other words, the relative risk of recidivism is greater for men with prior criminal court involvement for domestic violence, a finding that provides support for Hypothesis 2b.

Prior Court Involvement for Non-Domestic Violence Related Offenses and Recidivism of Domestic Violence

Hypothesis 2c states that the relative risk of recidivism for domestic violence related offenses is greater for men with prior criminal court involvement for non-domestic violence related offenses than for men with no prior criminal court involvement for non-domestic violence related offenses. Although the chi-square analysis demonstrates a statistically significant relationship between prior court involvement for non-domestic violence related offenses and recidivism, the multivariate model does not support Hypothesis 2c.

Legal Sanctions Dose-Response Index and Recidivism of Domestic Violence

Hypothesis 3 states that the hazard ratio for recidivism of domestic violence is greater for men with fewer legal sanctions for the index case, as measured by the Legal Sanctions Dose-Response Index. For the purposes of this research, dose-responses are the cumulative total of any protective order, arrest, probation, revocation, and incarceration applied as a legal sanction for the index case. One category was statistically significant: two legal sanctions (versus one legal sanction). Typically, this category includes a combination of arrest and probation; occasionally sanctions were limited to protective order and arrest. The results of the Cox PH regression model partially support Hypothesis 3.

Battering Intervention Program Participation and Recidivism of Domestic Violence

Hypothesis 4 proposes that the relative risk of recidivism for domestic violence related offenses is greater for men who did not complete a court-ordered battering intervention program than for men who completed a court-ordered battering intervention program. Despite a significant relationship between completion of a battering intervention program and recidivism found by the chi-square analysis, the multivariate model does not support Hypothesis 4.

Incarceration During the Follow-Up Period and Recidivism of Domestic Violence

Based on the premise that incarceration reduces opportunities to commit domestic violence offenses, Hypothesis 5 states that the hazard ratio for recidivism of domestic violence related offenses is negatively associated with the length of periods of incarceration for any criminal offenses committed after the index case. However, instead of an inverse relationship between the lengths of time incarcerated during the follow-up period and hazard ratio for recidivism, the hazards increase. The Cox proportional hazard regression model does not support Hypothesis 5.

SUMMARY

Of the 607 men in the sample, 184 men (30.3%) were involved with the courts for offenses that meet this study's definition of recidivism of domestic violence: civil court involvement for protective orders, or criminal court involvement for domestic violence related offenses between the date of index case offense and December 31, 2006. According to the Cox proportional hazard regression model, the findings are as follows:

- age is not associated with the hazard ratio for recidivism;
- race/ethnicity is not associated with risk of recidivism;
- prior civil court involvement for protective orders is not associated with the risk of recidivism;
- prior criminal court involvement for domestic violence related offenses is positively associated with the risk of recidivism;
- prior criminal court involvement for non-domestic violence related offenses is not associated with risk of recidivism;
- men with two sanctions (versus one) on the Legal Sanctions Dose-Response Index have lower hazards for recidivism;
- completion of a battering intervention program is not associated the relative risk of recidivism; and

- greater periods of incarceration for any criminal offenses committed after the index case are associated with greater hazard ratios for recidivism of domestic violence.

CHAPTER SEVEN

Discussion

Prior research findings on men who batter, legal responses to domestic violence, and recidivism of domestic violence are a study in contradictions. Age is a predictor of recidivism; age is not a predictor. Race/ethnicity is a predictor of recidivism; race/ethnicity is not a predictor. Prior criminal history is a predictor of recidivism; prior criminal history is not a predictor. There is a program effect of battering intervention program participation; there is no program effect of battering intervention program participation. This chapter discusses the results of the chi-square, the results of the *t*-test, and the results of the Cox proportional hazards regression analysis of the hypotheses. It also examines how the results of this study relate to prior research.

Based upon the sample of 607 men, there is a 30.3% recidivism rate for domestic violence related offenses in the county. The rate includes criminal cases filed in the county for domestic violence related offenses and any protective orders processed through the county's civil court between the date of the index case offense and December 31, 2006, approximately a five to six year period. Using official records, this is higher than other studies and less than rates found by other researchers. For example, one study found an 11.4% recidivism rate over a seven-year period for 70 men who participated in a battering intervention program (Lee, Uken, & Sebold, 2007). This recidivism rate is low in light of findings of other studies. Bouffard & Muftić (2007) found a 16% recidivism rate among domestic violence offenders over a 6 to 12 month follow-up period. With a follow-up period that ranged from 7 months to 58 months, Tollefson and Gross (2006) found a recidivism rate between 18% and 21% for 197 participants in a battering intervention program. Bowen, Gilchrist, and Beech (2005) found a 21% recidivism rate in their sample 86 men over an 11-month period following participation in a battering intervention program. Using arrest records, an evaluation of battering intervention programs linked to a misdemeanor court in Illinois assessed 899 men arrested for domestic violence and found a recidivism rate of 26.1% over 2.4 years (Bennett et. al, 2007). In sharp contrast, in a sample of 248 men, Gordon & Moriarty (2003) found an overall 47% re-arrest rate for domestic violence during one-year follow-up period.

There are several possible explanations for the differences in the recidivism rates between prior studies and this study. Unlike research which begins measuring recidivism following participation in a battering intervention program, this study measures recidivism from the date of the index case offense, which may have occurred up to a year or more before an individual is mandated to battering intervention. Hence, the window of opportunity to recidivate is larger. Nonetheless, the 30.3% recidivism rate found in this research may still be an underestimate of recidivism of domestic violence by the men in the sample. Police and sheriffs' departments within the county may not file all offenses that result in arrest with the District Attorney's office, and only cases filed with the county District Attorney's Office were available for review in the county databases. Arrest records and victims' statements at the time of arrest are not available in the county databases, but may provide additional information about recidivism of domestic violence. For example, Gondolf's research (2002) estimates a 49% cumulative recidivism rate during a four-year multi-site study of batterer intervention systems (Gondolf, 2002; Gondolf, 2004). Unlike this study, Gondolf did not rely solely upon court records for documentation of recidivism but included both perpetrators' and victims' reports of subsequent abuse through interviews conducted over a four-year period. Recidivism rates then may be a function of the operational definition of recidivism, the implementation of sanctions within the community under observation, the time the programs are under observation, and the individual characteristics of the offender.

Information about the individual circumstances, life experiences, and psychological characteristics of the offender is beyond the scope of this study. Regardless, the descriptive statistics indicate that there are differences between recidivists and non-recidivists in the sample of 607 men. For example, when compared to non-recidivists, recidivists in this study tend to be younger, are Black, and are more likely to have prior civil court involvement for protective orders, and prior criminal court involvement for both domestic and non-domestic violence related offenses.

Descriptive statistics also indicate that differences exist between recidivists and non-recidivists regarding their criminal court involvement for specific levels and types of offenses. Prior to the index case, recidivists are more likely to have been involved with the courts for felony level domestic violence and non-domestic violence related offenses against property and offenses against public administration such as retaliation, evading arrest, failure to register as a sex offender, and tampering with evidence. Recidivists are also more likely to have prior court involvement for misdemeanor offenses, specifically domestic violence and non-domestic violence related offenses against persons.

Compared to non-recidivists, recidivists are more likely to be court ordered to battering intervention through the civil courts for protective orders and are less likely to experience arrest for the index case. Once referred to a battering intervention program, recidivists are less likely than are non-recidivists to complete a program. Less than half of the men (40.5%) of the men in the sample contacted a battering intervention program. Of the 246 men who contacted a battering intervention program, 170 (69.1%) completed. The attrition rate for the men enrolled in battering intervention programs in the county was about 30.9%. Because so few men in the sample completed a battering intervention program (the completion rate was 28%), this study used additional analyses to determine if there were significant differences between men who did not complete battering intervention and men who did complete. The additional analyses indicate that the characteristics of recidivists who do not complete the battering intervention program are very similar to recidivists in the overall sample on most measures.

Researchers have found that men who do not comply with court ordered participation in a battering intervention program may be significantly different from those who complete a program in terms of individual characteristics and personal motivation (Bennett et al., 2007; Daly & Pelowski, 2000; Daly, Power, & Gondolf, 2001; Gondolf, 2004; Sartin, Hansen, & Huss, 2006). In their review of program attrition studies, Daly and Pelowski (2000) found that men who do not complete court ordered battering intervention are more likely to be unemployed, unmarried, without children, have lower incomes, and have less education than men who complete a program. Additionally, men who do not complete are more likely to have a criminal history and a history of substance abuse or related problems. Less understood are the characteristics of men who are court ordered to complete a battering intervention and are non-compliant with the court order.

To determine if any covariates predict how long the men in the sample are able to "survive" or maintain their non-recidivist status, this study tested the hypotheses using Cox proportional hazards regression analysis. The next section restates each hypothesis, presents the findings of the analysis related to each hypothesis, and discusses the implications of the findings from the analysis.

DEMOGRAPHICS AND RECIDIVISM

Hypothesis 1a. The hazard ratio for recidivism for domestic violence related offenses is negatively related to age at the time of the index case offense.

The results of the Cox proportional hazard regression model do not support Hypothesis 1a. Assuming that younger men would be more impulsive and reactive than older men, the results were unexpected. While the t-test determined that a significant difference exists between the mean ages of recidivists and non-recidivists, younger age as a risk factor for recidivism is not present in multivariate model. This is contrary to what some prior research has found (Babcock & Steiner, 1999; Bennett et al., 2007; Cissner & Puffett, 2006; Hanson & Wallace-Capretta, 2004; Klein & Crowe, 2008; Murphy, Musser, & Maton, 1998; Ventura & Davis, 2005). It is, however, consistent with some research which has found no significance (Bowen, Gilchrist, & Beech, 2005; Shepard, Falk, & Elliott, 2002).

Hypothesis 1b. The relative risk of recidivism for domestic violence related offenses is not associated with race or ethnicity.

The chi-square test indicates that significant differences exist between race and recidivism; recidivists were more likely to be Black men and less likely to be Hispanic men. However, further analysis indicates that the relative risk for recidivism is not associated with race or ethnicity. One possible explanation is that, whereas the bivariate analyses compared within race or ethnicity (i.e., Black men to Black men, Hispanic men to Hispanic men, and White men to White men), the multivariate analyses uses Black men as the reference group to which Hispanic and White men are compared. Nonetheless, the race or ethnicity of the men in the sample presents an interesting contrast to the general population of the county. While the population of adult men in the county during the timeframe of the study was predominantly White, the men in the sample are predominately Black and Hispanic men. In their study on domestic violence offenders and protective orders, Etter and Birzer (2007) found that Black men were overrepresented in their sample of accused offenders. In contrast, some studies have found that race has no influence on recidivism of domestic violence (Murphy, Musser, and Maton, 1998; Shepard, Falk, & Elliott, 2002; Ventura & Davis, 2005). Other research suggests that rates of domestic violence vary by the type of community for both Black men and White men and, for both groups, the rates of domestic violence are higher in the most disadvantaged community and lower in the least disadvantaged community. Additionally, the correlation between race and domestic violence is reduced or disappears completely when White men are compared to Black men in similar ecological contexts (Benson, Wooldredge, Thistlethwaite, & Fox, 2004). While it is beyond to scope of this study to examine ecological factors within the county, it is possible that the community context of the county influenced the race differential amongst the men in the sample. One potential explanation for the disproportionate number of Black men in the sample may be, for example, that race of the defendant influences the decision to prosecute and any subsequent sentencing decisions. In their research on prosecution effects, Hirschel and Hutchison (2001) found that, while not statistically significant, domestic violence cases were more likely to be prosecuted against Black defendants than White defendants were.

PRIOR COURT INVOLVEMENT AND RECIDIVISM

For the purposes of this study, prior court involvement for domestic violence included protective orders processed through the civil court and domestic violence related offenses disposed of through the criminal courts.

Hypothesis 2a. The relative risk of recidivism for domestic violence related offenses is greater for men with prior civil court involvement for protective orders than for men with no prior civil court involvement for protective orders.

This study finds that prior civil court involvement for protective orders does not increase the relative risk for recidivism of domestic violence. This is consistent with research that found that no one sanction, particularly a combination of arrest and protective order, was more effective than others in reducing recidivism of domestic violence (Mears et al., 2001). Using prior protective orders as a proxy for a history of domestic violence, another study found no significant relationship between prior protective orders and recidivism (Cissner & Puffett, 2006). However, the finding of the Cissner & Puffett study is unexpected; various studies estimate between 23% and 70% of protective orders are violated (Logan, Shannon, Walker, & Faragher, 2006), suggesting that recidivism of domestic violence related offenses would be an issue for men with prior court involvement for protective orders (Kingsnorth, 2006; Klein, 2008). It is not the case for the sample of 607 men in this study. It is possible that because this study uses official court records for the history of prior domestic violence related offenses (rather than victim reports of prior violations of protective orders), the impact of prior court involvement on civil protective orders is underestimated (Finn, 2003; Logan & Walker, 2009).

Hypothesis 2b. The relative risk of recidivism for domestic violence related offenses is greater for men with prior criminal court involvement for domestic violence related offenses than for men with no prior criminal court involvement for domestic violence related offenses.

As noted by Heckert and Gondolf (2000), increasing perceptions of criminal justice sanctions may not prevent recidivism. This study finds that the relative risk of recidivism is greater for those men who were involved with the criminal courts for any prior domestic violence related offenses, compared with men with no prior involvement, suggesting that one predictor of future behavior is past behavior. From a social learning perspective, it is possible that the recidivists in this study have learned to justify their violence towards their intimate partners (Bandura, 1979). While some studies found no relationship between prior arrests for domestic violence and recidivism (Bennett et al., 2007; Davis, Taylor, & Maxwell, 2000; Klein, 2008), this finding is consistent with a number of studies on recidivism of domestic violence (Bouffard & Muftić, 2007; Bowen, Gilchrist, & Beech, 2005; Davis, Smith, & Nickles, 1998; Kingsnorth, 2006; Klein & Tobin, 2008; Cissner & Puffett, 2006; Gordon & Moriarty; Rempel, Labriola, & Davis, 2008; Ventura & Davis, 2005). From the social exchange and deterrence perspectives, legal responses to domestic violence rely upon sanctions and the restraining function of punishment. The findings of this study suggest that for recidivists, legal sanctions for prior domestic violence and the index case were insufficient to stop their violence and may have had an "emboldening" effect, with punishment encouraging rather than deterring domestic violence (Piquero & Pogarsky, 2002). The number and type of prior sanctions for domestic violence related offenses and the sanctions for the index case may also encourage an emboldening effect. For example, Bouffard and Muftić (2007) suggest that lighter sentencing such as deferred sentences may undermine legal responses to domestic violence because offenders receiving deferred sentences may not feel the same threat of additional sanctions for non-compliance as do those not granted such deferments. Under such circumstances, it may not be appropriate for men with prior court involvement for domestic violence offenses to incur the same legal sanctions as those men without prior court involvement for domestic violence.

Hypothesis 2c. The relative risk of recidivism for domestic violence related offenses is greater for men with prior criminal court involvement for non-domestic violence related offenses than for men with no prior criminal court involvement for non-domestic violence related offenses.

The Cox proportional hazards regression model does not support Hypothesis 2c. The relative risk of recidivism was not significant for men with prior criminal court involvement for non-domestic violence related offenses, compared to men with none. This finding was unexpected because a number of studies have found that prior court involvement for non-domestic violence related offenses is a predictor of recidivism of domestic violence (Cissner & Puffett, 2006; Klein & Tobin, 2008; MacLeod et al., 2009; Rempel, Labriola, & Davis, 2008).

In this study, 59.0% of the 607 men in the sample had prior criminal court involvement for non-domestic violence related offenses. This percentage is well within the ranges found in other research on recidivism. According to Klein (2008), the percents of domestic violence perpetrators with a prior criminal history range from 49% in one study to as high as 84.4 percent in another.

LEGAL SANCTIONS DOSE-RESPONSE INDEX AND RECIDIVISM

Hypothesis 3. The hazard ratio for recidivism of domestic violence is greater for men with fewer legal sanctions for the index case, as measured by the Legal Sanctions Dose- Response Index.

For the purposes of this research, dose-responses include any civil protective order, arrest, probation, revocation, and incarceration applied as a legal sanction for the index case. The results of the Cox proportional hazards regression model are mixed. While a significant relationship exists between the imposition of two legal sanctions (versus one) and recidivism of domestic violence related offenses, the remaining combinations of legal sanctions are not statistically different from one sanction. The hazard ratio for recidivism is 45% lower for men who received two legal sanctions, relative to those with one legal sanction. As shown in Figure 1, those with two legal sanctions are able to maintain their non-recidivism status longer relative to those with one sanction.

The measure of one legal sanction is, in most cases, the imposition of a civil protective order. The combination of two legal sanctions typically includes arrest and probation. It is possible that because probation entails greater supervision and monitoring with more contacts with system than involvement with the civil court for protective orders, men on probation are less likely to recidivate (Murphy, Musser, & Maton, 1998).

BATTERING INTERVENTION PROGRAM COMPLETION AND RECIDIVISM

Hypothesis 4. The relative risk of recidivism for domestic violence related offenses is greater for men who did not complete a court-

ordered battering intervention program than for men who completed a court-ordered battering intervention program.

The results of the Cox PH regression model analysis do not support Hypothesis 4, and there is no difference in the relative risk for recidivism for men who completed a court ordered battering intervention program (versus those who did not complete a program). Additionally, there is no difference in the relative risk for recidivism for men who began a battering intervention program and terminated their participation before they completed. The analysis suggests that completion of a battering intervention program does not affect the length of time that men in the sample were able to maintain their non-recidivism status. Because more than two-thirds of the men court-ordered to attend a battering intervention program either did not contact (59.0%) or did not complete the battering intervention program (12.5%), it is possible that low participation rates affected the results of this analysis. Consistent with these results, some research has found little to no battering intervention program effect on recidivism (Davis, Taylor, & Maxwell, 2000; Feder & Dugan, 2002; Labriola, Rempel, & Davis, 2005; MacLeod et al., 2009). By contrast, and despite modest effect sizes and program limitations, including high participant attrition rates, some research indicates that men who complete battering intervention programs are less likely recidivate when compared to men who either drop-out of a program or simply do not attend (Babcock, Green, & Robie, 2004; Bennett et al., 2007; Gondolf, 2002; Gordon & Moriarty, 2003; Hendricks, Werner, Shipway, & Turinetti, 2006; Shepard, Falk, & Elliott, 2002). However, Maxwell, Davis, and Taylor (2010) suggest that battering intervention may have a suppression effect on recidivism rather than a treatment effect.

From a deterrence perspective, responses to non-compliance with court orders to participate in a battering intervention program could also influence program completion. It is unknown what sanctions, if any, the county courts instituted in response to non-compliance with the court order. For example, the criminal court may revoke probation due to non-compliance with the court ordered terms of probation. Grounds for revocation could be failure to complete a specific probation requirement related to the index case, such as court ordered completion of a battering intervention program. Technical violations, which could be non-compliance with any of the terms of probation, are also grounds for revocation (Rhodes et al., 2001). If the court requires time in jail as part of sentencing for the revocation, it is possible that incarceration will fulfill the terms of the probation and battering intervention program participation is no longer required (MacLeod et al., 2009). However, if there are little to no sanctions for non-compliance, then according to deterrence theory, the likelihood for recidivism increases (Piquero & Pogarsky, 2002).

Finally, it is beyond the scope of this study to examine the differences between battering intervention program completers and non-completers on an individual level. Each group may have different characteristics and motivations (Daly & Pelowski, 2000; Daly, Power, & Gondolf, 2001; Gondolf, 2004; Sartin, Hansen, & Huss, 2006; MacLeod et al., 2009). Considering the high non-compliance rate for battering intervention program participation in this sample of men, and the possibility of individual differences that may influence program participation, the results regarding battering intervention program participation are not conclusive.

OPPORTUNITY AND RECIDIVISM

Hypothesis 5. Because incarceration reduces opportunities for recidivism, the hazard ratio for recidivism of domestic violence related offenses is negatively associated with the length of periods of incarceration for any criminal offenses committed after the index case.

The Cox proporational hazard regression model analysis of the data does not support Hypothesis 5; the relative risk of recidivism and the length of time incarcerated after the index case are statistically significant and the hazard ratio is positively associated with the length of incarceration for any criminal offenses. There are two possible explanations. First, it is possible that the covariate "incarceration" is confounded with the dependent variable because the time spent incarcerated also includes incarceration for the offense that met the operational definition for recidivism. Of the recidivists in this study, 66.3% spent time incarcerated in jail or prison for varying lengths of time during the follow-up period for their recidivism. In essence, recidivists are at a greater risk to recidivate because their incarceration is due to recidivism. An alternative explanation is that the relative risk of recidivism is statistically significant and positively associated with incarceration because, rather than incarceration limiting opportunity, recidivists use whatever opportunity they have to commit domestic violence again once they are released from jail or prison.

SUMMARY

This study found a 30.3% recidivism rate for the 607 men in the study. The descriptive analyses found significant differences between recidivists and non-recidivists. Recidivists are more likely than are non-recidivists to be referred to battering intervention through the civil courts for protective orders and are less likely to be arrested for the index case. Compared to non-recidivists, recidivists tend to be younger, Black, and have prior court involvement for domestic violence offenses. When they recidivated, almost half of the recidivists committed felony level domestic violence offenses.

The hypotheses for this study factor in the element of time to recidivism or the hazard ratio or relative risk of recidivism. The analysis identifies three predictors of recidivism during the follow-up period: prior criminal court involvement for domestic violence related offenses, two legal sanctions (as opposed to one sanction), and incarceration during the follow-up period. Men with prior criminal court involvement for domestic violence related offenses are more likely to recidivate, suggesting that past behavior is a predictor of future behavior. It is also possible that legal sanctions imposed for prior domestic violence and for the index case were insufficient deterrents for recidivism of domestic violence. Using the Legal Sanctions Dose-Response Index, this study finds that the association between the hazard ratio for recidivism and two sanctions for the index case is negative. This suggests that the risk of recidivism is 45% lower for men who experienced two legal sanctions, relative to the reference group of men who experienced one legal sanction. Over two-thirds of the men on probation (72.6%, or 223 of 307 men) had terms of probation that were between 13 to 24 months. It is possible that greater supervision and monitoring afforded by probation contributes to reducing recidivism. Finally, rather than reducing opportunity to recidivate, longer periods of incarceration during the follow-up period for any offenses is a predictor of recidivism. However, the covariate "incarceration" may be confounded with the dependent variable because the time spent incarcerated during the follow-up period also includes incarceration for domestic violence offenses that meet the operational definition for recidivism. It is also possible that, rather than incarceration limiting opportunities, recidivists use whatever opportunities are available to them to commit domestic violence. Chapter Eight will discuss further implications of the results.

Summary and Conclusion

A distinction exists between the "personal troubles of milieu" and "public issues of social structure." Troubles are a private matter, occurring within the character of the individual and in relationships with others. Personal values held by the individual are threatened. Issues are a public matter where some value held in esteem by the public is threatened. Issues are located within the social and historical institutions of a society (Mills, 1959/2000). Vacillation between defining domestic violence as personal trouble or public issue is evident in historical and political efforts to address domestic violence in the United States.

This book presents four theoretical perspectives that inform criminal justice responses to domestic violence: social learning, social exchange/deterrence, feminist, and ecological (Danis, 2003). Because various levels of the ecological framework integrate social learning, social exchange/deterrence, and feminist theory into a formalized legal response (Danis, 2003), the discussion of the findings of this study is grounded within the county's response to domestic violence. Specifically, the discussion focuses on the broader scope of legal sanctions, treating domestic violence as a public issue within the context of the macrosystem of the county's rules and values demonstrated through sanctions imposed in response to domestic violence related offenses. Due to limitations in the data, not present in the discussion are the individual characteristics, motives, and personal values of the perpetrators that may influence recidivism.

This study examines the impact of legal sanctions among perpetrators of domestic violence. For the purposes of the study, legal sanctions for domestic violence include civil protective orders, arrest, probation, revocation, and incarceration. Comparing and contrasting recidivists and non-recidivists, the study considers prior court involvement for domestic violence and non-domestic violence related felony and misdemeanor offenses, post- index case court involvement for domestic violence and non-domestic violence related felony and misdemeanor offenses, and incarceration for any offenses committed during the follow-up period.

As noted in the introduction, this research explores three factors currently not addressed in the literature on men who batter women and who are court ordered to attend battering intervention. These factors are the cumulative effects of both civil and criminal legal sanctions (or dose-response of sanctions) for domestic violence related offenses on recidivism, reduced opportunities to recidivate, and if the number of legal sanctions imposed for the index case affects how long a man maintains his non-recidivist status.

In the multivariate analysis, this study uses the Legal Sanction Dose-Response Index to gauge the cumulative impact of sanctions imposed by the county civil and criminal courts upon recidivism of domestic violence. The risk of recidivism is 45% lower for men who experienced two legal sanctions (typically arrest and probation) in response to the index case, relative to men who experienced one legal sanction (typically civil protective order). In other words, those with two legal sanctions are able to refrain from recidivism longer relative to those with one sanction. It appears that the greater supervision and monitoring afforded by probation may contribute to reducing recidivism.

Rather than reducing opportunities to recidivate, longer periods of incarceration for any offenses committed during the follow-up period is a predictor of recidivism. As noted, incarceration during the follow-up period may be confounded because the time spent incarcerated includes incarceration for domestic violence offenses that meet the operational definition for recidivism. It is also possible that, rather than incarceration limiting opportunities, recidivists use whatever opportunities are available to them to commit domestic violence, despite legal sanctions. Gondolf (2002) found that approximately 20% of the men in his multi-site evaluation repeatedly assaulted their partners during the four-year follow-up and were responsible for the most severe violence. It is possible that for this sample of men, recidivists incarcerated during the follow-up period are similarly persistent and resistant to sanctions.

Considering the factor of the length of time that men in the sample maintained their non-recidivism status, the multivariate analysis identifies three significant predictors related to recidivism: prior criminal court involvement for domestic violence, the imposition of two legal sanctions, and incarceration during the follow-up period. Simply, men with prior criminal court involvement for domestic violence related offenses are more likely to recidivate, indicating that past behavior is a predictor of future behavior. Additionally, prior civil court involvement for protective orders approached statistical significance and it may be a factor to consider in future research. It is possible that past legal sanctions for prior domestic violence related offenses combined with sanctions for the index case were insufficient deterrents for recidivism of domestic violence for a distinct group of men. Indeed, the findings suggest that it may not be appropriate for men with prior civil or criminal court involvement for domestic violence offenses to incur the same legal sanctions as those men without prior court involvement for domestic violence.

There were significant bivariate differences between recidivists and non-recidivists in the sample. About 59% of the men in the sample were involved with the courts for non-domestic violence related offenses prior to the index case. A statistically significant bivariate association exists between prior court involvement for non-domestic violence related offenses and recidivism. In contrast, the multivariate analysis indicates that the length of time men in the sample maintained their non-recidivism status is not affected by prior court involvement for non-domestic violence related offenses. Does this finding mean that consideration of court involvement for prior non-domestic violence related offenses is not useful when evaluating risk of recidivism? The mixed results indicate that enough evidence exists to be concerned and spur additional research in this area of study.

For approximately 60% of the recidivists, the index case was through the civil court for protective orders, suggesting that civil sanctions for domestic violence offenses (the only sanction imposed for 44% of the sample of 607 men) may have reduced deterrence effects when compared to those who are involved with the criminal courts. One possible reason may be that, because the sanction is civil and not criminal, there is no court-imposed monitoring to ensure compliance with the court order. Failure to participate in court-ordered battering intervention is a violation of the civil court order and courts have the option of imposing criminal sanctions. Although criminal sanctions are the most frequently used means used to enforce protective orders (United States Department of Justice, 2002), it is beyond the scope of this study to determine the legal sanctions imposed by the county for non-compliance with the civil protective order. Continuing research should examine the efficacy of civil protective orders and particularly community responses to non-compliance with conditions of protective orders.

A similar situation arises with court ordered participation in a battering intervention program. Of the 607 men in the study, fully 72% did not contact or complete court ordered battering intervention. Breaking down the percentages, 59.5% did not contact a program and 12.5% began a program but did not complete. A significant bivariate association exists between completion of a battering intervention program and recidivism, with more non-recidivists completing a program. Further bivariate analyses found that recidivists attend fewer hours of battering intervention. However, the multivariate analyses suggest completion of a battering intervention program does not affect the length of time that men in the sample were able to maintain their non-recidivism status. Although the findings are mixed, the interpretation of the results does not imply that battering intervention programs are ineffective. Additional research should investigate those men who are court ordered to attend battering intervention and yet do not contact or complete a battering intervention program. What are the ramifications of their non-compliance and how does the community deal with them?

In their discussion of past evaluations of coordinated community response demonstration programs, Garner and Maxwell (2008) note initial findings of no differences in rates of domestic violence between jurisdictions with coordinated responses and jurisdictions without coordinated responses. However, they recommend using caution in interpreting the findings as a basis for reducing the level of support for efforts to improve coordination in the delivery of services to victims. The same caution applies to interpreting the results of this study as a basis for rejecting the use of sanctions such as civil protective orders or reducing referrals to battering intervention for domestic violence related offenses.

FUTURE RESEARCH

Do cumulative legal sanctions have an emboldening effect on men who commit domestic violence? Compared to non-recidivists, recidivists are more likely to be court referred to battering intervention through the civil courts for protective orders and are therefore less likely to experience arrest for the index case. Once referred, recidivists are less likely than are non-recidivists to complete a battering intervention program, suggesting that compliance with the court order to participate in a battering intervention program is not perceived as important by those who eventually recidivate. Additionally, combining prior civil court involvement for protective orders and prior criminal court involvement for domestic violence related offenses, approximately 86.4% of the recidivists in this study had come to the attention of the county courts for domestic violence prior to the index case. For these men, the offense that constituted recidivism was, at the minimum, their third involvement with a county court for domestic violence related offenses. It appears that additional sanctions for a core group of men are insufficient to stop their violent behaviors directed toward their intimate partners. Future research should focus on those men who appear to be at greater risk for recidivism, and determine if specialized interventions are necessary. According to Wilson and Klein (2006), when men are persistent in their criminal behaviors, as some of the men in this study appear to be, legal sanctions cannot be expected to be successful. Paradoxically, in these cases, substantial jail or prison terms may be the sanction required to increase public safety.

The Legal Sanction Dose-Response Index is a useful tool to conceptualize and recognize the imposition of single and multiple sanctions for one case of domestic violence. The rationale behind the Legal Sanction Dose-Response Index is that there are multiple sanctions that may be imposed for one case, yet (with rare exceptions, such as Mears et al., 2001) most of the research does not consider civil and criminal sanctions combined for intervention in domestic violence cases. Although the Dose-Response Index was useful in this study for evaluating multiple sanctions, in the end, for those men in the sample who received one legal sanction for the index case, the case was typically disposed of through the civil court for protective orders. For those men who received two sanctions for the index case, the case was typically disposed of through the criminal court and the sanctions were arrest and probation. This suggests two future areas for research. One area of future research is to examine the risk of recidivism for those who receive civil protective orders for the index case. Future research should also consider civil protective orders in combination with other legal sanctions imposed for cases, including criminal sanctions. Although not statistically significant, those with one sanction imposed (typically civil protective order) were more likely to recidivate than those who received criminal court sanctions. Knowing more about this population would add to the body of research on civil protective orders and their efficacy for protecting victims of domestic violence.

Would victim reports of recidivism have increased the 30.3% recidivism rate found in this study? Although one goal of legal sanctions is victim safety, research regarding criminal justice responses to domestic violence rarely takes into consideration victims' experiences (Fleury, 2002; Ford, 1999). Unfortunately, this is also the case for this study. For example, the dependent variable recidivism is defined as civil court involvement for protective orders, or criminal court involvement for domestic violence related offenses between the date of index case and December 31, 2006. The measure is broad compared to other research because it includes both protective order cases and criminal cases, whether or not there was a conviction. In contradiction, the measure is also very narrow because it confines recidivism to "involvement with the court." The length of time a man maintained his non-recidivism status is not necessarily an indication that men in the sample did not commit domestic violence after the index case. It is an indication that some cases that constituted recidivism captured the attention of the legal system within the county. Taking into consideration additional measures such as victims' reports of re-abuse during the follow-up period, researchers tend to find higher rates of recidivism, which could be a more accurate representation of the experience of victims and efficacy of legal sanctions (Davis, Taylor, & Maxwell, 2000; Gondolf, 2002; Labriola, Rempel, & Davis, 2005).

Domestic violence is unique as a crime in that the perpetrator typically has privileged access to the victim over time, particularly if there are children (Logan, Shannon, Walker, & Faragher, 2006; Stark, 2006). Of great concern in the current study is the level of criminal domestic violence related offenses during the follow-up period. Almost half of the recidivists in this study (48.9%) were involved with the courts after the index case for domestic violence related felony offenses such as murder, attempted murder, kidnapping, aggravated assault, sexual assault, and use of a deadly weapon. One of the limitations of this study is that it did not consider the number of protective orders granted or the number of criminal cases filed during the follow-up period, nor did it consider the level of offense that met the definition of recidivism. Frequencies of protective orders and criminal cases may have provided more insight into the persistence of some men in the sample to be domestically violent. Future research should further examine if there is an escalation of abuse over time or if those who more violent are a different population from most of the men who are involved with the civil courts for protective orders or criminal courts for misdemeanor domestic violence related offenses.

CONCLUSION

Because prior court involvement for domestic violence is a significant factor in recidivism of domestic violence, and because recidivists are at greater risk for incarceration during the follow-up period, the results suggest that a subset of men is resistant to standard legal sanctions and persistent in their commission of domestic violence related offenses. Learning more about and addressing this subset of men is one critical element to reducing domestic violence.

In his 2002 book, Gondolf poses the following relevant questions. How does a community's response to domestic violence contribute to changes in public attitudes, and external institutional responses? What indicates success? What values esteemed by the community does domestic violence threaten? Do the cultural norms and values, and the reduction of violence within a community reflect the community's response to domestic violence (Gondolf, 2002)? Statutes, law enforcement responses, prosecutorial policies and procedures, probation monitoring protocols, battering intervention program structures, and data collection systems develop organically and are idiosyncratic to a community. More broadly, in order to treat domestic violence as a public issue of social structure, communities must move beyond defining domestic violence as a personal trouble, expand the conceptualization beyond civil and criminal sanctions, which equate domestic violence with discrete episodes in time (Stark, 2006), and examine and establish cultural norms and values that support nonviolence.

References

Adler, M. A. (2002). The utility of modeling in evaluation planning: The case of coordination of domestic violence services in Maryland. *Evaluation and Program Planning, 25*, 203-213.

Allen, N. E. (2006). An examination of the effectiveness of domestic violence coordinating councils. *Violence Against Women 12*(1), 46-67.

Allison, P. D. (1999). *Multiple regression: A primer.* Thousand Oaks, CA: Pine Forge Press.

Altman, D. G. (1991). *Practical statistics for medical research.* New York: Chapman & Hall.

Babcock, J. & Steiner, R. (1999). The relationship between treatment, incarceration, and recidivism of battering: A program evaluation of Seattle's Coordinated Community Response to domestic violence. *Journal of Family Psychology, 13*, 46-59.

Babcock, J., Green, C. E., & Robie, C. (2004). Does batterers' treatment work? A meta-analytic review of domestic violence treatment. *Clinical Psychology Review, 23*, 1023-1053.

Bailey, J. (2006). 'I dye [sic] by Inches': Locating wife beating in the concept of a privatization of marriage and violence in eighteenth-century England. *Social History, 31*(3), 273-294.

Bair-Merritt, M. H., Crowne, S. S., Thompson, D. A., Sibinga, E., Trent, M., & Campbell, J. (2010). Why do women use intimate partner violence? A systematic review of women's motivation. *Trauma, Violence, & Abuse, 11*(4), 178-189.

Bandura, A. (1969). Social learning theory of identificatory processes. In D. A. Goslin (Ed.), *Handbook of socialization theory and research* (pp. 213-262). Chicago: Rand McNally.

Bandura, A. (1973). *Aggression: A social learning analysis.* Englewood Cliffs, NJ: Prentice Hall.

Bandura, A. (1979). The social learning perspective: Mechanisms of aggression. In H. Toch (Ed.), *Psychology of crime and criminal justice* (pp. 198-236). New York: Rinehart & Winston.

Barnett, O. W. & Lee, C. Y., & Thelen, R. E. (1997). Gender differences in attributions of self-defense and control in interpartner aggression. *Violence Against Women, 3*(5), 462-482.

Beesley, F. & McGuire, J. (2009). Gender-role identity and hypermasculinity in violent offending. *Psychology, Crime & Law, 15*(2-3), 251-268.

Belsky, J. (1980). Child maltreatment: An ecological integration. *American Psychologist, 35*(4), 320-335.

Bennett, L. W., Stoops, C., Call, C. & Flett, H. (2007). Program completion and re-arrest in a batterer intervention system. *Research on Social Work Practice, 17*(1), 42-54.

Benson, M. L., Wooldredge, J., Thistlethwaite, A. B., & Fox, G. L. (2004). The correlation between race and domestic violence is confounded with community context. *Social Problems, 51*(3), 326-342.

Berk, R. A., & Newton, P. N. (1985). Does arrest really deter wife beating? An effort to replicate the findings of the Minneapolis Spouse Abuse Experiment. *American Sociological Review, 50,* 253-262.

Berk, R. A., Campbell, A., Klap, R., & Western, B. (1992). The deterrent effect of arrest on incidents of domestic violence: A Bayesian analysis of four field experiments. *American Sociological Review, 51,* 698-708.

Bern, E. H. (1985). Domestic violence: Some theoretical issues related to criminal behavior. *Journal of Applied Social Sciences, 9*(2), 136-147.

Bevacqua, M. & Baker, C. (2004). "Pay no attention to the man behind the curtain!": Power, privacy, and the legal regulation of violence against women. *Women and Politics, 26*(3/4), 57-83.

Blau, P. M. (1964). *Exchange and power in social life.* New York: John Wiley & Sons.

Bograd, M. (1988). Feminist perspectives on wife abuse: An introduction. In K. Yllö & M. Bograd (Eds.), *Feminist perspectives on wife abuse* (pp. 11-26). Newbury Park, CA: Sage.

Bouffard, J. A. & Muftić, L. R. (2007). An examination of the outcomes of various components of a coordinated community response to domestic violence by male offenders. *Journal of Family Violence, 22,* 353-366.

Bourdieu, P. (2001). *Masculine domination.* (R. Nice, Trans.) Stanford, CA: Stanford University Press.

Bowen, E., Gilchrist, E. A., & Beech, A. R. (2005). An examination of the impact of community-based rehabilitation on the offending behavior of male domestic violence offenders and the characteristics associated with recidivism. *Legal and Criminological Psychology, 10,* 189-209.

Boyle, D. J., O'Leary, K. D., Rosenbaum, A., Hassett-Walker, C. (2008). Differentiating between generally and partner-only violent subgroups: Lifetime antisocial behavior, family of origin violence, and impulsivity. *Journal of Family Violence, 23,* 47-55.

Bradburn, M. J., Clark, T. G., Love, S. B., & Altman, D. G. (2003). Survival analysis part II: Multivariate data analysis - an introduction to concepts and methods. *British Journal of Cancer, 89,* 431-436.

Brennan, P. A., & Mednick, S. A. (1994). Learning theory approach to the deterrence of criminal recidivism. *Journal of Abnormal Psychology, 103*(3), 430-440.

Brewer, J. D. (2003). *C. Wright Mills and the ending of violence.* New York: Palgrave MacMillan.

Bronfenbrenner, U. (1977). Toward an experimental ecology of human development. *American Psychologist, 32,* 523-531.

Bronfenbrenner, U. (1986). Ecology of the family as a context for human development: Research perspectives. *Developmental Psychology, 22*(6), 732-742.

Burt, M. R., Harrell, A. V., Newmark, L. C., Aron. L. Y., Jacobs, L. K. and others (1997). *Evaluation guidebook for projects funded by S. T. O. P. formula grants under the Violence Against Women Act.* Washington D. C.: Urban Institute.

Buzawa, E. S. & Buzawa, C. G. (2003). *Domestic violence: The criminal justice response* (3rd ed.) Thousand Oaks, CA: Sage.

Carlson, M. J., Harris, S. D., & Holden, G. W. (1999). Protective orders and domestic violence: Risk factors for re-abuse. *Journal of Family Violence, 14*(2), 205-226.

Carmody, D. C. & Williams, K. R. (1987). Wife assault and perceptions of sanctions. *Violence and Victims 2*(1), 25-38.

Case, P. F. (2008). The relationship of race and criminal behavior: Challenging cultural explanations for a structural problem. *Critical Sociology, 34*(2), 213-238.

Cissner, A. B. & Puffett, N. K. (2006). *Do batterer program length or approach affect completion or re-arrest rates? A comparison of outcomes between defendants sentenced to two batterer programs in Brooklyn.* Retrieved from the Center for Court Innovation website: http://www.courtinnovation.org/_uploads/documents/IDCC_DCA P%20final.pdf

Clark, T. G., Bradburn, M. J., Love, S. B., & Altman, D. G. (2003). Survival analysis part I: Basic concepts and first analyses. *British Journal of Cancer, 89,* 232-238.

Cohen, J. (1992). A power primer. *Psychological Bulletin, 112*(1), 155-159.

Cosimo, S. D. (1999, July). *Research affects policy affects programs: The need for context.* Paper presented at the Sixth International Family Violence Research Conference, University of New Hampshire, Durham, NH.

Daly, J. E. & Pelowski, W. (2000). Predictors of dropout among men who batter: A review of studies with implications for research and practice. *Violence and Victims, 15*(2), 137-160.

Daly, J. E., Power, T. G., & Gondolf, E. W. (2001). Predictors of batterer program attendance. *Journal of Interpersonal Violence, 16*(10), 971-991.

Danis, F. S. (2003). The criminalization of domestic violence: What social workers need to know. *Social Work, 48*(2), 237-246.

Dasgupta, S. D. (1999). Just like men? A critical view of violence by women. In M. Shepard & E. Pence (Eds.), *Coordinating community responses to domestic violence: Lessons from Duluth and beyond* (pp. 195-222). Thousand Oaks, CA: Sage.

Dasgupta, S. D. (2002). Framework for understanding women's use of nonlethal violence in intimate heterosexual relationships. *Violence Against Women, 8*(11), 1364-1389.

Davis, R. C., Smith, B. E., & Nickles, L. B. (1998). The deterrent effect of prosecuting domestic violence misdemeanors. *Crime & Delinquency, (44)*3, 434-442.

Davis, R., Taylor, B., & Maxwell, C. (2000). *Does batterer treatment reduce violence? A randomized experiment in Brooklyn.* Washington, DC: National Institute of Justice.

Dobash, R. E. (2003). Domestic violence: Arrest, prosecution, and reducing violence. *Criminology and Public Policy, 2*(2), 313-318.

Dobash, R. P. & Dobash, R. E. (1981). Community response to violence against wives: Charivari, abstract justice and patriarchy. *Social Problems, 28*(5), 563-581.

Douglas, U., Bathrick, D., & Perry, P. A. (2008). Deconstructing male violence against women: The Men Stopping Violence community – accountability model. *Violence Against Women, 14*(2), 247-261.

Durkheim, E. (1997). *The division of labor.* New York: Free Press. (Original work published in 1893).

Dutton, D. G. (1995). *The domestic assault of women: Psychological and criminal justice perspectives.* Vancouver: UBC Press.

Edelson, J. L. & Tolman, R. M. (1992). *Intervention for men who batter: An ecological approach.* Newbury Park, CA: Sage.

Emmers-Sommer, T. M., Pauley, P., Hanzal, A, & Triplett, L. (2006). Love, suspense, sex, and violence: Men's and women's film predilections, exposure to sexually violent media, and their relationship to rape myth acceptance. *Sex Roles,* 55, 211-320.

Etter, G. W., & Birzer, M. L. (2007). Domestic violence abusers: A descriptive study of characteristics of defenders in protection from abuse orders in Sedgwick County, Kansas. *Journal of Family Violence, 22,* 113-119.

Feder, L., & Dugan, L. (2002). A test of the efficacy of court-mandated counseling for domestic violence offenders: The Broward experiment. *Justice Quarterly, 19*(2), 343-375.

Finn, M. A. (2004). *Effects of victim's experiences with prosecutors on victim empowerment and reoccurrence of intimate partner violence, final report* (NIJ Publication No. 202983). Retrieved from http://www.ncjrs.gov/pdffiles1/nij/grants/202983.pdf

Fletcher, A. (1994). Men's dilemma: The future of patriarchy in England 1560-1660. *Transactions of the Royal Historical Society, Sixth Series,* (4), 61-81.

Fleury, R. E. (2002). Missing voices: Patterns of battered women's satisfaction with the criminal justice system. *Violence Against Women, 8*(2), 181-205.

Ford, D. A. (1999, July). *Coercing victim participation in domestic violence prosecutions.* Paper presented at the Sixth International Family Violence Research Conference, University of New Hampshire, Durham, NH.

Forde, D. R., & Kennedy, L. W. (1997). Risky lifestyles, routine activities, and the General Theory of Crime. *Justice Quarterly, 14*(2), 265-294.

Foster-Fishman, P. G., Nowell, B., Yang, H. (2007). Putting the system back into systems change: A framework for understanding and changing organizational and community systems. *American Journal of Community Psychology, 39,* 197-215.

Frost, L. A. (2006). A forensic evaluator's guide to the Texas legal system. *Applied Psychology in Criminal Justice, 2*(3), 5-28.

Garner, J. H. & Maxwell, C. D. (2008). Coordinated community responses to intimate partner violence in the 20th and 21st centuries. *Criminology & Public Policy, 4*(4), 525-535.

Garson, G. D. (2008a). Cox regression. *Statnotes: Topics in Multivariate Analysis.* Retrieved from http://faculty.chass.ncsu.edu/garson/pa765/statnote.htm.

Garson, G. D. (2008b). Student's t-test of difference of means. *Statnotes: Topics in Multivariate Analysis.* Retrieved from http://faculty.chass.ncsu.edu/garson/pa765/statnote.htm.

Gelles, R. J. (1979). *Family Violence.* Beverly Hills, CA: Sage.

Gelles, R. J. (1982). Applying research on family violence to clinical practice. *Journal of Marriage and the Family, 44*(1), 9-20.

Gelles, R. J. (1983). An exchange/social control theory. In D. Finkelhor, R. J. Gelles, G. T. Hotaling, & M. A. Straus (Eds.), *The dark side of families: Current family violence research* (pp. 151-165). Beverly Hills, CA: Sage.

Gelles, R. J. (1993). Through a sociological lens: Social structure and family violence. In R. J. Gelles & D. R. Loske (Eds.), *Current controversies in family violence* (pp. 31-46). Newbury Park, CA: Sage.

Gimenez, M. E. (1975). Marxism and feminism. *Frontier: A Journal of Women's Studies, 1*(1), 61-80.

Gondolf, E. W. (2002). *Battering intervention systems: Issues, outcomes, and recommendations.* Thousand Oaks, CA: Sage.

Gondolf, E. W. (2004). Evaluating batterer counseling programs: A difficult task showing some effects and implications. *Aggression and Violent Behavior, 9,* 604-631.

Goode, W. J. (1971). Force and violence in the family. *Journal of Marriage and the Family, 33*(4), 634-636.

Gordon, J. A. & Moriarty, L. J. (2003). The effects of domestic violence batterer treatment on domestic violence recidivism: The Chesterfield county experience. *Criminal Justice and Behavior, 30*(1), 118-134.

Gover, A. R., Jennings, W. G., Davis, C., Tomsich, E. A., Tewksbury, R. (2011). Factors related to the completion of domestic violence offender treatment: The Colorado experience. *Victims and Offenders, 6,* 137-156.

Grissom, R. J., & Kim, J. J. (2005). *Effect sizes for research: A broad practical approach.* Mahwah, NJ: Erlbaum.

Hamberger, L. K. (1997). Female offenders in domestic violence: A look at actions in their contexts. *Journal of Aggression, Maltreatment, & Trauma, 1,* 117-129.

Hamberger, L. K., & Guse, C. E. (2002). Men's and women's use of intimate partner violence in clinical samples. *Violence Against Women, 8*(11), 1301-1331.

Hamberger, L. K., Lohr, J. M., Bonge, D., & Tolin, D. F. (1997). An empirical classification of motivations for domestic violence. *Violence Against Women, 3*(4), 401-424.

Hamby, S. L. (1998). Partner violence: Prevention and intervention. In J. L. Jasinski & L. M. Williams (Eds.), *Partner violence: A comprehensive review of 20 years of research.* Thousand Oaks, CA: Sage.

Hamilton, M., & Worthen, M. G. F. (2011). Sex disparities in arrest outcomes for domestic violence. *Journal of Interpersonal Violence, 26*(8), 1559-1578.

Hansen, M. (1993). Feminism and family therapy: A review of feminist critiques of approaches to family violence. In M. Hansen & M. Harway (Eds.), *Battering and family therapy: A feminist perspective.* Newbury Park, CA: Sage.

Hanson, R. K., & Wallace-Capretta, S. (2004). Predictors of criminal recidivism among male batterers. *Psychology, Crime & Law, 10*(4), 413-427.

Healey, K., Smith, C., & O'Sullivan, C. (1998). *Batterer intervention: Program approaches and criminal justice strategies.* Washington, DC: National Institute of Justice.

Heckert, D. A. & Gondolf, E. W. (2000). The effect of perceptions of sanctions on batterer program outcomes. *Journal of Research in Crime and Delinquency, 37*(4), 369-391.

Heise, L. L. (1998). Violence against women: An integrated, ecological framework. *Violence Against Women, 4*(3), 262-290.

Hendricks, B., Werner, T., Shipway, L., Turinetti, G. J. (2006). Recidivism among spousal abusers: Predictions and program evaluation. *Journal of Interpersonal Violence, 21*(6), 703-716.

Henning, K., & Feder, L. (2004). A comparison of men and women arrested for domestic violence: Who presents the greater threat? *Journal of Family Violence,* 19(2), 69-80.

Hines, D. A., & Douglas, E. M. (2009). Women's use of intimate partner violence against men: prevalence, implications, and consequences. *Journal of Aggression, Maltreatment & Trauma, 18,* 572-586.

Hines, D. A., & Malley-Morrison, K. (2005). *Family violence in the United States: Defining, understanding, and combating abuse.* Thousand Oaks, CA: Sage.

Hirschel, D., and Hutchison, I. W. (2001). The relative effects of offense, offender, and victim variables on the decision to prosecute domestic violence cases. *Violence Against Women, 7*(1), 46-59.

Hirschel, D., Hutchison, I. W., & Shaw, M. (2010). The interrelationship between substance abuse and the likelihood of arrest, conviction, and re-offending in cases of intimate partner violence. *Journal of Family Violence, 25,* 81-90.

Irving, M. (2002). Domestic Violence. *The Georgetown Journal of Gender and the Law: Fourth Annual Review of Gender and Sexuality Law, 4*(1), 453-488.

Jasinski, J. L. (2001). Theoretical explanations for violence against women. In C. M. Renzetti, J. L. Edleson, and R. K. Bergen (Eds.), *Sourcebook on violence against women.* Thousand Oaks, CA: Sage.

Jerrell, J. M. & Ridgely, M. S. (1999). The relative impact of treatment program 'robustness' and 'dosage' on client outcomes. *Evaluation and Program Planning, 22,* 323-330.

Jewell, L. M. & Wormith, J. S. (2010). Variables associated with attrition from domestic violence treatment programs targeting male batterers: A meta-analysis. *Criminal Justice and Behavior*, 37(10), 1086-1113.

Jones, A. S., D'Agostino, R. B., Gondolf, E. W., & Heckert, A. (2004). Assessing the effect of batterer program completion on reassault using propensity scores. *Journal of Interpersonal Violence, 19*(9), 1002-1020.

Johnson, R. R. (2008). Correlates of re-arrest among felony domestic violence probationers. *Federal Probation, 72*(3), 42-47.

Keiley, M. K., & Martin, N. C. (2005). Survival analysis in family research. *Journal of Family Psychology, 19*(1), 142-156.

Keilitz, S. L., Davis, C., Efkeman, H. S., Flango, C., & Hannaford, P. L. (1998). *Civil protection orders: Victim's views on effectiveness.* Washington, DC: Department of Justice (NIJ No. FS000191).

Keilitz, S. L., Hannaford, P. L., & Efkeman, H. S. (1997). *Civil protection orders: The benefits and limitations for victims of domestic violence.* National Center for State Courts Research Report, NCSC Publications Number: R-201. Williamsburg, VA.

Kernsmith, P. & Kernsmith, R. (2009). Treating female perpetrators: State standards for battering intervention services. *Social Work, 54*(4), 341-349.

Kethineni, S., & Beichner, D. (2009). A comparison of civil and criminal orders of protection as remedies for domestic violence victims in a midwestern county. *Journal of Family Violence, 24*, 311-321.

Kingsnorth, R. (2006). Intimate partner violence: Predictors of recidivism in a sample of arrestees. *Violence Against Women, 12*(10), 917-935.

Klein, A. R. & Crowe, A. (2008). Findings from an outcome examination of Rhode Island's specialized domestic violence probation supervision program: Do specialized supervision programs of batterers reduce reabuse? *Violence Against Women, 14*(2), 226-246.

Klein, A. R. (2008). *Practical implications of current domestic violence research. Part III: Judges.* Washington, DC: National Institute of Justice.

Klein, A. R., & Tobin, T. (2008). A longitudinal study of arrested batterers, 1995 – 2005: Career criminals. *Violence Against Women, 14*(2), 136-157.

Labriola, M., Bradley, S., O'Sullivan, C. S., Rempel, M., & Moore, S. (2009). A national portrait of domestic violence courts. Retrieved from http://www.ncjrs.gov/pdffiles1/nij/grants/229659.pdf.

Labriola, M., Rempel, M., & Davis, R. (2005). *Testing the effectiveness of batterer programs and judicial monitoring: Results from a randomized trial at the Bronx misdemeanor domestic violence court.* Retrieved from Center for Court Innovation website: http://www.courtinnovation.org/_uploads/documents/battererprogr amseffectiveness.pdf.

Labriola, M., Rempel, M., O'Sullivan, C. S., Frank, P. B., McDowell, J., & Finkelstein, R. (2007). *Court responses to batterer program noncompliance: A national perspective.* Retrieved from http://www.ncjrs.gov/pdffiles1/nij/grants/230399.pdf

Lawson, D. M., Brossart, D. F., & Shefferman, L. W. (2010). Assessing gender role of partner-violence men using the Minnesota multiphasic personality inventory-2 (MMPI-2): Comparing abuser types. *Professional Psychology: Research and Practice, 41*(3), 260-266.

Lee, M. Y., Uken, A., Sebold, J. (2004). Accountability for change: Solution-focused treatment with domestic violence offenders. *Families in Society: The Journal of Contemporary Social Services, 85*(4), 463-476.

Logan, T. K. & Walker, R. (2009). Civil protective order outcomes: Violations and perceptions of effectiveness. *Journal of Interpersonal Violence, 24*(4), 675-692.

Logan, T. K. & Walker, R. (2010). Civil protective order effectiveness: Justice or just a piece of paper? Violence and Victims, 25, 332-348.

Logan, T. K., Shannon, L., Walker, R., & Faragher, T. M. (2006). Protective orders: Questions and conundrums. *Trauma, Violence, & Abuse, 7*(3), 175-205.

MacLeod, D., Pi, R., Smith, D., Rose-Goodwin, L. (2009). *Batterer intervention systems in California: An evaluation.* Retrieved from Office of Court Research, Administrative Office of the Courts website: http://www.courtinfo.ca.gov/reference/batintsys.htm.

Malley-Morrison, K. & Hines, D. A. (2004). *Family violence in a cultural perspective: Defining, understanding, and combating abuse.* Thousand Oaks, CA: Sage.

Manning, P. K. (1993). The preventive conceit: The black box in market context. *American Behavioral Scientist, 36*(5), 639-650.

Massachusetts (1890). *A bibliographical sketch of the laws of the Massachusetts Colony from 1630 to 1686. In which are included the Body of Liberties of 1641, and the records of the Court of Assistants, 1641-1644. Arranged to accompany the reports of the Laws of 1660 and of 1672.* Boston, MA: Rockwell and Churchill City Printers.

Maxwell, C. D., Davis, R. C., & Taylor, B. G. (2010). The impact of length of domestic violence treatment on the patterns of subsequent intimate partner violence. *Journal of Experimental Criminology, 6,* 475-497.

Maxwell, C. D., Garner, J. H., & Fagan, J. A. (2001). *The effects of arrest on intimate partner violence: New evidence from the Spouse Assault Replication Program.* Washington, DC: National Institute of Justice.

McCarroll, J. E., Thayer, L. E., Liu, X., Newby, J. H., Norwood, A. E., Fullerton, C. S., & Ursano, R. J. (2000). Spouse abuse recidivism in the U. S. army by gender and military status. *Journal of Consulting and Clinical Psychology, 68*(3), 521-525.

Mears, D. P., Carlson, M. J., Holden, G. W., & Harris, S. D. (2001). Reducing domestic violence revictimization: The effects of individual and contextual factors and type of legal intervention. *Journal of Interpersonal Violence, 16*(12), 1260-1283.

Mederos, F. (1999). Batterer intervention programs: The past and future prospects. In M. F. Shepard & E. L. Pence (Eds.), *Coordinating community responses to domestic violence: Lessons from Duluth and beyond.* Thousand Oaks: Sage Publications.

Michalski, J. H. (2004). Making sociological sense out of trends in intimate partner violence: The social structure of violence against women. *Violence Against Women, 10*(6), 652-675.

Michalski, J. H. (2005). Explaining intimate partner violence: The sociological limitations of victimization studies. *Sociological Forum, 20*(4), 613 – 640.

Mill, J. S. (1970). *The subjection of women.* Cambridge, MA: M.I.T. Press. (Original work published in 1869).

Mill, J. S. (1975). *On Liberty.* (D. Spitz, Ed.). New York, NY: Norton & Company. (Original work published 1859).

Millett, K. (1971). *Sexual politics.* New York, NY: Avon.

Mills, C. W. (2000). *The sociological imagination.* New York, NY: Oxford University Press. (Original work published in 1959).

Mirchandani, R. (2006). "Hitting is not manly": Domestic violence court and the re-imagination of the patriarchal state. *Gender & Society, 20*(6), 781-804.

Molm, L. D. (1994). Is punishment effective? Coercive strategies in social exchange. *Social Psychology Quarterly, 57*(2), 75-94.

Morao, K. (2006). Domestic violence and the state. *Georgetown Journal of Gender & the Law, 2006 Annual Review of Gender and Sexuality Law, 7*(3), 787-817.

Mowrer, H. (1937). Clinical treatment of marital conflicts. *American Sociological Review, 2*(5), 771-778.

Muftić, L. R. & Bouffard, J. A. (2007). An evaluation of gender differences in the implementation and impact of a comprehensive approach to domestic violence. *Violence Against Women, 13*(1), 46-69.

Murphy, C. M., Musser, P. H., & Maton, K. I. (1998). Coordinated community intervention for domestic abusers: Intervention system involvement and criminal recidivism. *Journal of Family Violence, 13,* 263-284.

Olivero, J. M. (2010). How is domestic violence defined for therapeutic purposes? *National Social Science Journal, 34*(2), 110-128.

O'Neill, P. (2005). The ethics of problem definition. *Canadian Psychology/Psychologie Canadiennne, 46,* 13-20.

Olson, D. E. & Stalans, L. J. (2001). Violent offenders on probation: Profile, sentence, and outcome differences among domestic violence and other violent probationers. *Violence Against Women, 7*(10), 1164-1185.

Olver, M. E., Stockdale, K. C., & Wormith, J. S. (2011). A meta-analysis of predictors of offender treatment attrition and its relationship to recidivism. Journal of Consulting and Clinical Psychology, 79(1), 6-21.

Payne, B. K. & Gainey, R. R. (2005). *Family violence and criminal justice: A life-course approach* (2ⁿᵈ ed.). New York: Anderson Publishing

Pence, E., & Paymar, M. (1993). *Education groups for men who batter: The Duluth Model.* New York, NY: Springer.

Peterson, R. R., & Dixon, J. (2005). Court oversight and conviction under mandatory and nonmandatory domestic violence case filing policies. *Criminology & Public Policy, (4)*3, 353-558.

Petrucci, C. J. (2010). A descriptive study of a California domestic violence court: Program completion and recidivism. *Victims and Offenders*, 5, 130-160.

Piquero, A. R., & Paternoster, R. (1998). An application of Stafford and Warr's reconceptualization of deterrence to drinking and driving. *Journal of Research in Crime and Delinquency,* 35, 3-39.

Piquero, A. R., & Pogarsky, G. (2002). Beyond Stafford and Warr's reconceptualization of deterrence: personal and vicarious experiences, impulsivity, and offending behavior. *Journal of Research in Crime and Delinquency, 39*(2), 153-186.

Pleck, E. (1989). Criminal approaches to family violence, 1640-1980. *Crime and Justice, 11,* 19-57.

Pleck, E. (2004). *Domestic tyranny: The making of American social policy against family violence from colonial times to the present.* Urbana, IL: University of Illinois Press.

Portwood, S. G. & Heany, J. F. (2007). Responding to violence against women: Social science contributions to legal solutions. *International Journal of Law and Psychiatry, 30,* 237-247.

Post, L. A., Klevens, J., Maxwell, C. D., Shelley, G. A., & Ingram, E. (2010). An examination of whether coordinated community responses affect intimate partner violence. *Journal of Interpersonal Violence, 25*(1), 75-93.

Rajan, M., & McCloskey, K. A. (2007). Victims of intimate partner violence: Arrest rates across recent studies. *Journal of Aggression, Maltreatment & Trauma,15*(3/4), 27-52.

Rawls, J. & Kelly, E. (2001). *Justice as fairness: A restatement.* Cambridge: Harvard University Press.

Ray, J. (1768). *A compleat collection of English proverbs: Also the most celebrated proverbs of the Scotch, Italian, French, Spanish, and other languages. The whole methodically digested and illustrated with annotations, and proper explanations.* Printed for W. Otridge, S. Bladon. Original from the University of Michigan. Digitized December 20, 2005. Retrieved from http://books.google.com.

Rempel, M., Labriola, M., & Davis, R. C. (2008). Does judicial monitoring deter domestic violence recidivism?: Results of a quasi-experiment comparison in the Bronx. *Violence Against Women, 14*(2), 185-207.

Rhodes, W., Pelissier, B., Gaes, G., Saylor, W., Camp, S., & Wallace, S. (2001). Alternative solutions to the problem of selection bias in an analysis of federal residential drug treatment programs. *Evaluation Review, 25*(3), 331-369.

Rossi, P. H., Freeman, H. E., & Lipsey, M. W. (1999). *Evaluation: A systematic approach* (3rd. ed.). Thousand Oaks, CA: Sage.

Rousseve, A. (2005). Domestic violence and the state. *Georgetown Journal of Gender & the Law, 2005 Annual Review of Gender and Sexuality Law, 6*(3), 431-458.

Salazar, L. F., Emshoff, J. G., Baker, C. K., & Crowley, T. (2007). Examining the behavior of a system: An outcome evaluation of a coordinated community response to domestic violence. *Journal of Family Violence, 22,* 631-641.

Sartin, R. M., Hansen, D. J., Huss, M. T. (2006). Domestic violence treatment response and recidivism: A review and implications for the study of family violence. *Aggression and Violent Behavior, 11,* 425- 440.

Saurage Research Report (2003). *Prevalence, perceptions and awareness of domestic violence in Texas: A quantitative study conducted for the Texas Council on Family Violence.* Office of the Texas Attorney General.

Seamans, C. L., Rubin, L. J., & Stabb, S. D. (2007). Women domestic violence offenders: Lessons of violence and survival. *Journal of Trauma & Dissociation, 8*(2), 47-68.

Shepard, M. (1999). Evaluating coordinated community responses to domestic violence. In M. Shepard & E. Pence (Eds.), *Coordinating community responses to domestic: Lessons from Duluth and beyond.* Thousand Oaks, CA: Sage.

Shepard, M. (2005). Twenty years of progress in addressing domestic violence: An agenda for the next 10. *Journal of Interpersonal Violence, 20*(4), 436-441.

Shepard, M. F. & Pence, E. L. (1999). *Coordinating community responses to domestic violence: Lessons from Duluth and beyond.* Thousand Oaks, CA: Sage.

Shepard, M., Falk, D. R., & Elliot, B. A. (2002). Enhancing coordinated community responses to reduce recidivism in cases of domestic violence. *Journal of Interpersonal Violence, 17*(5), 551-569.

Sherman, L. W. & Berk, R. A. (1984). The specific deterrent effects of arrest for domestic assault. *American Sociological Review, 49*(2), 261-272.

Sherman, L. W., Smith, D. A., Schmidt, J. D., & Rogan, D. P. (1992). Crime, punishment, and stake in conformity: Legal and informal control of domestic violence. *American Sociological Review, 57*(5), 680-690.

Sitren, A. H. & Applegate, B. K. (2007). Testing the deterrent effects of personal and vicarious experience with punishment and punishment avoidance. *Deviant Behavior, 28*, 29-55.

Smith, D. E. (1987). *The everyday world as problematic: A feminist sociology.* Boston, MA: Northeastern University Press.

Snell, J. E., Rosenwald, R. J., and Robey, A. (1964). The wife-beater's wife. *Archives of General Psychiatry, 11*, 107-112.

Stafford, M. C. & Warr, M. (1993). A reconceptualization of general and specific deterrence. *Journal of Research and Delinquency, 30*(2), 123-135.

Stark, E. (2006). Commentary on Johnson's "Conflict and control: Gender symmetry and asymmetry in domestic violence." *Violence Against Women, 12*(11), 1019-1025.

Stone, D. (2002). Using knowledge: The dilemmas of 'bridging research and policy.' *Compare: A Journal of Comparative Education, 32*(3), 285-296.

Straus, M. A. (2009). Current controversies and prevalence concerning female offenders of intimate partner violence: Why the overwhelming evidence on partner physical violence by women has not been perceived and is often denied. *Journal of Aggression, Maltreatment & Trauma, 18*, 552-572.

Taylor, B. G., Davis, R.C., & Maxwell, C.D. (2001). The effects of a group batterer treatment program in Brooklyn. *Justice Quarterly, 18*, 170-201.

Texas Code of Criminal Procedure, Title 1, Chapter 14, Article 14.03(a)(4) and (b).

Texas Department of Criminal Justice- Community Justice Assistance Division and Texas Council on Family Violence. (1999). *Battering Intervention and Prevention Project Guidelines.* Retrieved from http://www.tcfv.org/pdf/guidelines.pdf

Texas Department of Public Safety. (2000). *Crime in Texas: 2000.* Uniform Crime Reporting, Crime Information Bureau, and Crime Records Service.

Texas Family Code, Section 71.004. Family violence. (2007)

Texas Family Code, Chapter 85.022. Requirements of order applying to person who committed family violence. (2007).

Texas Penal Code, Title 5 – Title 9. (2007).

Thistlethwaite, A., Wooldredge, J., & Gibbs, D. (1998). Severity of dispositions and domestic violence recidivism. *Crime & Delinquency, 44*(3), 388-398.

Toch, H. (1992). *Violent men: An inquiry into the psychology of violence.* Washington, DC: American Psychological Association.

Tollefson, D. R. & Gross, E. R. (2006). Predicting recidivism following participation in a treatment program for batterers. *Journal of Social Service Research, 32*(4), 39-62.

Townsend, M., Hunt, D., Kuck, S., & Baxter, C. (2006). *Law enforcement response to domestic violence calls for service.* Washington, DC: National Institute of Justice.

Turner, J. H. (1998). *The structure of sociological theory* (6th. ed.). Belmont, CA: Wadsworth Publishing Company.

Ulmer, J. T. (2001). Intermediate sanctions: A comparative analysis of the probability and severity of sanctions. *Sociological Inquiry, 71*(2), 164-93.

United States Census Bureau (2000). *Census 2000 Summary File 3 (SF 3).* Retrieved from http://factfinder.census.gov.

United States Department of Justice (2002). *Enforcement of protective orders: Legal series bulletin No. 4.* (NCJ Publication No. 189190). Retrieved   from http://www.ojp.usdoj.gov/ovc/publications/bulletins/legalseries/bulletin4/ncj189190.pdf

Ventura, L. A. & Davis, G. (2005). Domestic violence: Court case conviction and recidivism. *Violence Against Women, 11*(2), 255-277.

Vogel, L. (1983). *Marxism and the oppression of women: Toward a unitary theory.* New Brunswick, NJ: Rutgers University Press.

Weber, M. (1946). The social psychology of the world religions. In H. H. Gerth, & C. W. Mills (Eds. & Trans.), *From Max Weber: Essays in sociology* (pp. 267-301). New York: Oxford University Press. (Original work published in 1922-3).

Weiss, C. H. (1998). *Evaluation: Methods for studying programs and policies* (2nd ed.). Upper Saddle River, NJ: Prentice Hall.

Weiss, J. A. (1989). The powers of problem definition: The case of government paperwork. *Policy Sciences, 22,* 97-121.

Williams, K. R. & Hawkins, R. (1986). Perceptual research on general deterrence: A critical review. *Law & Society Review, 20*(4), 545-572.

Williams, K. R. (2005). Arrest and intimate partner violence: Toward a more complete application of deterrence theory. *Aggression and Violent Behavior, 10,* 660-679.

Wilson, D. & Klein, A. (2006). *A longitudinal study of a cohort of batterers arraigned in a Massachusetts District Court 1995 to 2004.* Washington, DC: National Institute of Justice.

Wolfgang, M. E., & Ferracuti, F. (2001). *The subculture of violence: Towards an integrated theory in criminology.* New York: Routledge. (Original work published in 1967).

Woo, J. (2002). Domestic Violence. *The Georgetown Journal of Gender and the Law: Third Annual Review of Gender and Sexuality Law, 3*(2), 559-593.

Wooldredge, J. (2007). Convicting and incarcerating felony offenders of intimate assault and the odds of new assault charges. *Journal of Criminal Justice, 35,* 379-389.

Wooldredge, J., & Thistlethwaite, A. (2005). Court dispositions and rearrest for intimate assault. *Crime & Delinquency (51)*1, 75-102.

Yllö, K. A. (1993). Through a feminist lens: Gender, power and violence. In R. J. Gelles & D. R. Loske (Eds.), *Current controversies in family violence* (pp. 47-62). Newbury Park, CA: Sage.

Yodanis, C. L. (2004). Gender inequality, violence against women, and fear: A cross-national test of the feminist theory of violence against women. *Journal of Interpersonal violence, 19*(6), 655-675.

Zorza, J. (1992). The criminal law of misdemeanor domestic violence, 1970-1990. *Journal of Criminal Law and Criminology, 83*(1), 46-72.

Index